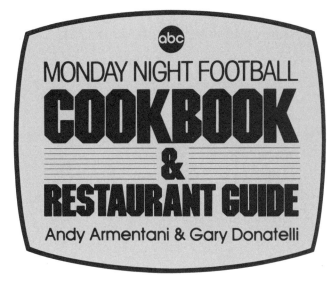

abc

MONDAY NIGHT FOOTBALL

COOKBOOK

&

RESTAURANT GUIDE

Andy Armentani & Gary Donatelli

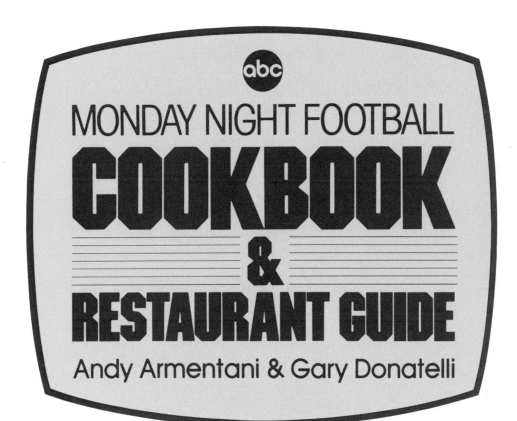

abc
MONDAY NIGHT FOOTBALL
COOKBOOK
&
RESTAURANT GUIDE

Andy Armentani & Gary Donatelli

CHILTON
BOOK COMPANY
RADNOR, PENNSYLVANIA

Copyright © 1982 by Andy Armentani and Gary Donatelli
All Rights Reserved
Published in Radnor, Pennsylvania 19089, by Chilton Book Company
and simultaneously in Canada by VNR Publishers,
1410 Birchmount Road, Scarborough, Ontario M1P 2E7

Manufactured in the United States of America
Designed by Naughton Studios

Library of Congress Cataloging in Publication Data
Main entry under title:

The Monday night football cookbook and
restaurant guide.

Includes index.
1. Cookery, International.   2. Restaurants,
lunch rooms, etc.—United States—Directories.
3. National Football League.
I. Armentani, Andy, 1925–   II. Donatelli, Gary, 1951–
TX725.A1M64   1982   641.5   82-71965
ISBN 0–8019–7270–1 (pbk.)

Photo credits
Cover: front panel, Jim Conroy; back panel, ABC Sports
Color Insert: page 1, Jim Conroy; page 2, The Greater New Orleans
Tourist and Convention Commission; page 3, top — the author,
center — ABC Sports, bottom — the author; page 4, the author;
page 5, top — Jim Conroy, bottom — the author; page 6, top — the
author, bottom — ABC Sports; page 7, top — Jim Conroy, bottom
— ABC Sports; page 8, all by ABC Sports.

FOREWORD
BY DON MEREDITH

Being Jeff and Hazel's baby boy and Billy Jack's little brother, I have the simplest of tastes. I always prefer the best. My two favorite foods are chicken fried steak and caviar. One tells you where I'm from. The other, where I've been.

There is a lot of room to explore between chicken fried steak and caviar. Over the past 11 years as a member of the Monday Night Football crew, we have all shared, in ABC tradition, a quest for the finest food and drink in NFL cities — coast to coast.

Traditionally, the dining table has been the setting for friends and families gathering at the end of each day to relax, share, and laugh with loved ones. Even holidays are distinguished by foods from Birthday cakes and turkeys to Easter eggs.

One of the highlights of my travels with the Monday Night Football organization is enjoyment of friendship around a table laden with food and drink.

It has been exciting and rewarding to educate our palates through the impeccable guidance of Andy Armentani and Gary Donatelli, whose ideas and notebooks have resulted in this book. In the following pages, you'll find a guide to the restaurants where our friendships have flourished and our waistlines expanded — along with many of the recipes that made the occasions special. I hope you'll enjoy with your friends.

CONTENTS

ACKNOWLEDGMENTS

There were many people who helped us in many different ways on this, our first book. We'd like to thank David, Blair, and Catherine Crabtree, whose book *A la San Francisco* helped formulate the idea for ours; Roone Arledge, Erwin Weiner (our Godfather), Tony Rezza and Denise Shapiro from ABC, who helped us work within the company; the editing and design staff at Chilton; David Spungen for finding the legal help necessary; Jim and Clair Mendiola of Abbreviated Word, Inc. for turning notes into a manuscript; Drew and Robyn DeRosa for using their home as a test kitchen; Debra Zalkind for keeping things together at home for us while we traveled; Don Meredith for a wonderful Foreword; and all our friends at work and across the country whose recipes filled our book, and whose meals filled our stomachs.

Our schedule allows us only so much time in each city and, because of this, we may have missed a great restaurant or local recipe that you feel should be included. We'd be glad to visit your favorite restaurant or try a specialty for the next edition of the *Monday Night Football Cookbook and Restaurant Guide*. Please send your suggestions or recipes to: Monday Night Football Cookbook and Restaurant Guide, #14G, 752 West End Avenue, New York, NY 10025.

INTRODUCTION

What do two sports cameramen know about writing a restaurant guide and cookbook? For starters, we spend some two hundred days a year away from home covering "con-

Photo by ABC Sports

stant variety of sport." Traveling the *Monday Night Football* tour alone takes us to some twenty cities across the U.S. each year.

One of the benefits of being on the road is sampling cuisine from the different regions and ethnic influences that make up this country. One of the problems of being on the road is that trying new places can sometimes end up in disappointment or, worse, indigestion. After years of trial and error, Andy began to fill a notebook with names of restaurants that consistently offered good service, atmosphere and, most important, food. Having been treated to many a fine meal, Gary thought the notebook would be of interest to many people who traveled for a living as we did, or who traveled just for pleasure. The plan was expanded to include recipes from the establishments, so whether one traveled or not, the variety of dishes could be prepared at home.

The U.S. has been called "the melting pot" of the world because so many nationalities resettled here. We have tried to select a good cross-section of restaurants to represent these influences, as well as influences that climate, region, and food sources have on local dishes. The recipes range from gourmet to gourmand, and the restaurants range from four star to "fast bite and a beer." Two things they all have in common is good service and good food.

When the rest of the crew discovered we were serious about this book, we were amazed to find they had so many terrific suggestions; so, we've included a special section featuring their favorites. After all, we have to eat with these folks!

This book, then, is an expansion of the original notebook, done — as Howard would say — "the ABC way." If you're a traveler, we hope this book will serve you well. If you're a homebody, we guarantee these recipes are so delicious they could pull a football fan away from the TV on a Sunday afternoon. And hey, that way football will be watched when it should be: on Monday night!

Enjoy,
Andy Armentani and
Gary Donatelli

PART I

Photo by ABC Sports

PRO FOOTBALL CITIES:
FAVORITE RESTAURANTS & RECIPES

ATLANTA

Atlanta has been the "center of the South" since before the Civil War. Some of the traditional dishes from that time can still be found today. One place that never seems to change in this city of change is *Mary Mac's Tea Room*. The Lupo family still makes things the old way. If you want to "put a little South in your mouth," this is the place. "Chicken Dumplings," "Brunswick Stew," "Black-Eyed Peas with Salt Pork," and "Sweet Potato Soufflé" can be all yours for half of what you would expect to pay—and that includes cornbread and sweetened ice tea, Southern style. It's not a fancy place, just good home cookin' and nice people for a great price.

Atlanta, "center of the New South," reflects another set of eateries. The last fifteen years have brought many people from the North who are attracted by the milder climate and growing business. Sidney Glazer, a northern transplant, has a nice little place in the North end of town called *Sidney's Just South*. If you stop in you'll find a cozy little house with soft music, "a place for lovers," as Sid says. A local told us that Sidney's Just South wasn't named because it was slightly southern; rather it was named that because the house was south of the Pancake House on Roswell Road. Well, the Pancake House is gone, but Sidney's is still serving fine food. It's an unassuming place outside, but a warm, casual gourmet restaurant inside. Fran Tarkenton, no stranger to Atlanta, swears by it.

The Pleasant Peasant is another cozy place. It was so successful downtown that they built a new place uptown in Buckhead, called *The Peasant Uptown*. Since then the Peasant, Inc. has opened *The Country Place*, *The Public House*, and *Dailey's*. All are excellent restaurants for food, service and atmosphere. The new place, Dailey's, seems to be the "in place" now, although each place has loyal clientele.

Bugatti, featuring the city's largest Italian wine selection, is in The Omni International Hotel complex downtown. It could be called the "Nouvelle Northern Italian," not just another Italian restaurant. If you want your taste buds and stomach to really love you, try their Sunday Brunch. The green velvet booths are comfortable and most of the staff are from Italy.

If soul food is your thing, Will Sanders, our resident expert, says the collard greens and chitlins at the *Chitlin King*, a few blocks southeast of Atlanta's Fulton County Stadium, are a must.

At the stadium, the Falcons have been serving something the fans just love—"Grits Blitz."

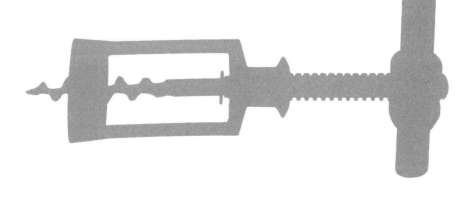

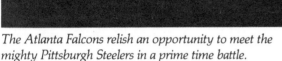

ATLANTA

The Atlanta Falcons relish an opportunity to meet the mighty Pittsburgh Steelers in a prime time battle.

BRUNSWICK STEW

Mary Mac's Tea Room

1 16-oz. can tomatoes
1 cup whole-grain corn
½ cup onion, chopped
1 cup chicken, cooked
1 cup pork, cooked
½ cup beef, cooked
Salt, pepper and Worcestershire sauce, to taste
½ cup barbecue sauce
hot sauce
Aćcent

☐ In heavy pot, mash up tomatoes. Add whole-grain corn and onion. Cook slowly together.

Grind together cooked chicken, pork and beef. Add to tomato mix. Season with salt, pepper, Worcestershire, hot sauce, barbecue sauce, dash of Aćcent.

Simmer very slowly about one hour. Serve with barbecued pork; makes 4 to 6 servings.

LUCKSCHEN KUGEL

Sidney's "Just South"

1 lb. egg noodles (any size)
4 eggs
1½ sticks butter

⅙ tsp. salt
¼ cup sugar
⅛ tsp. cinnamon
dash lemon

☐ Boil noodles according to instructions on package. Drain in colander, pour a little cold water over and drain again. Let stand. Meanwhile melt all the butter in a pan you will use for baking kugel. (A 9 x 12-in. baking pan should do the job.)

Beat the eggs in a large bowl, add noodles, sugar, salt, raisins, cinnamon, lemon, and melted butter. Leave plenty of butter in pan. Be sure to taste the noodles, to make sure the taste is right for your liking. You may need to add a little bit more of a lacking ingredient to acquire the right taste. Bake 40 minutes at 350° F. Serves 4 to 6.

SWEET POTATO SOUFFLÉ

Mary Mac's Tea Room

4 yams
oleo
whole milk
2 eggs
salt, to taste
sugar, to taste
pecans, coconut, or pineapple (optional)

☐ Boil yams. Skin, and mash well.

Add melted oleo, and whole milk, enough to make the mix rather soupy. Add salt and sugar to taste. Then beat eggs, stir into the sweet potato mix, pour into buttered baking dish, and bake at 325°F., about 30 minutes.

Pecans may be added, or coconut, or pineapple.

After the soufflé has set up or raised in the oven, add marshmallows on top, and brown. Serves four.

TROTELLA ALLA SAVOIA
(Baked Trout with Mushrooms)

Bugatti

6 10-oz. rainbow trout
1 lb. fresh mushrooms, sliced
4 oz. white wine
1 bunch green onions, sliced
4 oz. olive oil
4 oz. flour
2 oz. butter
juice of 2 fresh lemons
salt and pepper, to taste

☐ Season trout with salt and pepper, and dredge in flour. Sauté in olive oil until brown on both sides and remove. Drain off oil. Add butter and sautéed mushrooms. Add wine and lemon juice. Place trout on top of mushrooms. Sauté green onions in butter lightly and pour on top of trout. Bake in oven for 10 minutes at 375°F. or until done.

SCALLOP PARISIENNE

The Pleasant Peasant

2 T. butter, clarified
6 oz. fresh scallops
¼ cup white sauce
white wine, as needed
Parmesan bread crumbs

☐   Melt butter and clarify. Place butter in frying pan. Heat. Add scallops and enough wine to cover. Sauté until scallops are done. Remove from heat and drain. Place in individual serving dish and top with white sauce. Sprinkle with Parmesan bread crumbs. Place under broiler to brown, then serve immediately. Yields 1 serving.

CHOCOLATE WALNUT PIE

The Peasant Public House

6 T. butter
1½ cup sugar
¾ cup flour
3 large eggs
1½ cup walnuts, chopped
1½ cup semi-sweet chocolate chips
2 tsp. vanilla
1 unbaked pie shell, chilled

☐   Preheat oven to 350° F.

Break eggs into a bowl and whip lightly. Continue whipping and add sugar. Whip in melted butter, then vanilla. Stir in flour, then chocolate chips and nuts. Fill pie shell.

Bake 40-45 minutes until filling is fairly firm and crust is light brown. Chill.

Serve with whipped cream or vanilla ice cream. Garnish with chopped walnuts, chocolate shavings, and a spoonful of crème de cocoa. Yields one pie, 8 servings.

WHITE GAZPACHO

The Peasant Country Place

2 cups dry, white wine
4 cups chicken broth
½ cup lemon juice, freshly squeezed
1 bunch scallions
1 bunch parsley
3 cucumbers, large
3 tomatoes
dash Tabasco
salt, to taste
½ tsp. white pepper

☐   Bring the wine, chicken broth and lemon juice to a boil. Chill several hours or overnight.

Chop scallions and parsley. Slice cucumbers, and roughly chop tomatoes. Combine all ingredients and add to chilled soup. Taste for seasonings.

MARINATED CHICKEN LIVERS

The Peasant Public House

Marinade

2 T. apple cider vinegar
2 T. lemon juice
1 tsp. garlic salt
½ tsp. white pepper
½ tsp. dry mustard
1 cup vegetable oil

Livers

2 pt. (2–2½ lb.) chicken livers
1½ tsp. salt
½ tsp. black pepper
½ cup flour
2 T. oil (more if needed)
2 green peppers
3 cherry tomatoes, per serving
lettuce, for garnish

☐   Prepare the marinade: combine all ingredients except oil in a blender or food processor and blend for 30 seconds.

Gradually add the oil in a stream and blend until smooth. Refrigerate until needed.

Mix flour, salt and pepper in a shallow pan. Dredge livers in the flour. Heat oil in a skillet over medium heat. Sauté livers a few at a time until they stiffen. Turn them over and continue to cook about 2 minutes until firm but still pink inside. Julienne the green pepper and combine with the livers. Pour dressing over and marinate several hours or overnight in the refrigerator.

To serve: place livers on leaf lettuce and garnish with 3 cherry tomatoes. Makes 1 cup of marinade for 6 servings of liver.

TORTELLINI ALLA CREMA
(Tortellini in Cream Sauce)

Bugatti

2 lb. tortellini
1 pt. heavy cream
2 oz. butter
2 oz. flour
1 oz. white wine
2 oz. Parmesan cheese
¼ tsp. shallots, chopped
⅛ tsp. garlic, chopped
salt and pepper, to taste
1 oz. parsley, chopped

☐   Sauté shallots and garlic in butter. Add wine and reduce by half. Add flour to make roux. Add boiling cream and stir until smooth. Season, add parsley, and simmer for 10–15 minutes. Add cooked tortellini in cream and pour into serving dish. Garnish with Parmesan cheese.

Photo by the author

SWEET AND SOUR CABBAGE

Sidney's "Just South"

Meat mixture
2 lb. ground chuck, lean
2 eggs (beaten with a little salt)
1 carrot, grated
1 T. salt
1/8 tsp pepper
2 T. onion soup mix
2 T. ketchup
1 cup water

Sauce
1 15-oz. can tomato sauce
1 8-oz. can tomato sauce
1/6 tsp. salt
1/8 tsp. pepper
2 ginger snaps
1/2 cup brown sugar

1/4 cup raisins
1 fresh lemon

Cabbage
1 head large green cabbage
6 qt. boiling water

☐ Put up a 6-quart pot of water to boil. When water is boiled, add cored cabbage to loosen leaves, then take leaves out one by one with prongs. Put in colander, drain with a little cold water running on cabbage, and set aside.

Sauce

☐ In a 6-quart pot, put tomato sauce, salt, and pepper. Bring to a boil, then turn down heat and let it simmer. Add ginger snaps, raisins, brown sugar, squeeze half a lemon and let it cook slowly.

Meanwhile prepare the ground meat mixture. Sample the meat for the right taste.

Fill cabbage leaves with ground meat mixture—about a heaping tablespoon in each leaf—and roll up. Put the rolls in the sauce and bring to a fast boil. Then cook on slow boiling point for about two hours. Taste the sauce while cooking about every half hour to make sure you get the right sweet and sour taste. You may have to add more sugar or lemon and maybe a dash of salt. Serves 6.

CORNISH HENS

The Peasant Uptown

4 Cornish hens (one per person)

Stuffing
2 cups rice, cooked
1/2 tsp. cinnamon
1/2 tsp. basil
1/2 tsp. nutmeg
1/3 cup raisins
1/4 cup mushrooms, chopped
4 artichoke hearts (one per hen)
1 apple, quartered

☐ Combine stuffing ingredients.
Stuff each hen and place one apple quarter and one artichoke in each.
Roast at 375° F. for 1-1½ hours.
Serve with wine sauce (see below).

Wine Sauce
2 cups brown sauce
1/2 cup red wine
1 tsp. basil
1/2 tsp. cinnamon
1/2 tsp. nutmeg

☐ Bring to a boil.

1/4 cup sliced mushrooms
1/4 cup raisins

Add mushrooms and raisins, then reduce heat to a simmer. Simmer 15 minutes, then serve over hens.

ALMOND NEAPOLITAN

The Peasant Uptown

Crust

1 lb. vanilla wafer crumbs
1 cup almonds, toasted, slivered
½ cup sugar
¼ lb. margarine, melted

Filling

1 pt. coffee ice cream
2 pt. chocolate ice cream
1 pt. cinnamon ice cream
1 cup almonds, toasted, slivered

Sauce

¾ cup honey
¾ cup Amaretto liqueur
¼ tsp. cinnamon

☐ Grind wafers into crumbs. Chop almonds into small pieces (1 cup).

Combine crumbs, almonds, sugar and melted margarine. Mix well. Pat into springform pan—on bottom and halfway up sides. Bake at 350° F. for 15 minutes.

To fill pie, spread chocolate ice cream on outer edge of pan. Mound coffee ice cream into center of ring. Cover coffee ice cream with mound of cinnamon. Sprinkle with 1 cup toasted almonds, then freeze. Pour sauce over before serving.

BAGNA CAUDA
(Hot Anchovy and Garlic Dip)

Bugatti

1 green pepper
1 zucchini
2 carrots
4 celery stalks
1 cucumber
½ cauliflower
1 bunch broccoli flowerets
½ lb. fresh mushrooms
breadsticks

Sauce (Dip)

¼ lb. butter
¼ tsp. garlic, chopped
4 anchovy filets, finely chopped
7 cups heavy cream
1 cup fish stock
¼ cup wine

☐ Cut vegetables into 2 x ½-in. strips. Arrange on a platter around small bowl.

For the dip, melt butter in a small casserole over low heat. Add anchovy, garlic, fish stock, and wine and cook for about two minutes. Add cream and let simmer until the sauce is reduced to about 1½ cups. Do not let the sauce boil.

HONEY BAKED ONIONS

Mary Mac's Tea Room

6 white, sweet medium-sized onions, Vidalias if available
1½ cups tomato juice
1½ cups water
6 tsp. melted oleo
6 tsp. honey

☐ Peel and trim onions. Cut in half and place in buttered baking pan. Mix other ingredients and pour over onions. Bake 1 hour at 325°F., or until soft. Serves 6.

CHICKEN PERLOO

Mary Mac's Tea Room

In large heavy skillet, combine:
1 cup chicken broth
1 cup celery slices
1 cup onion slices
1 cup bell pepper strips
1 garlic clove, chopped
1 small piece jalapeno pepper

> Cook slowly 10 minutes.
> Add: 1 bay leaf

¼ tsp. marjoram
¼ tsp. leaf thyme
½ tsp. salt
½ tsp. parsley
1 qt. hot water
1 cup raw rice
1 cup knockwurst, sliced
1 cup tomatoes, peeled and sliced
2 cups chicken, cooked and chopped

☐ Cook slowly ½ hour. Add tomato juice if mixture gets dry. Serve with chopped peanuts on top. Serves 4.

Photo by the author

BALTIMORE

Baltimore brings to mind two things for us: crabcakes and Frank Gifford. Crabcakes because the Chesapeake Bay abounds with seafood—oysters, clams, and a whole lot of crabs. In Baltimore, crabcakes are almost more famous than Johnny Unitas. Frank Gifford comes to mind because he played with the New York Giants back when the Baltimore Colts and the Giants had one of the most famous rivalries in pro football history. What do crabcakes and the Giffer have in common? You can find both of them in the press box on Monday night in Baltimore.

If you like crab, you've come to the right city. You can choose from crabcakes, stone crab, crab fingers, stuffed crab, crab imperial Chesapeake or, if you really want to go native, soft shell crab sandwiches (deep-fried whole crabs between two pieces of bread).

According to the *Baltimore Sun* newspaper, as well as *Baltimore* magazine, *Thompson's Sea Girt House* has "Baltimore's Best Crabcake." The food at Thompson's is so popular that anything on the menu can be packaged for carry-out. They'll package and ship the crabcakes anywhere in quantities from a half dozen to hundreds, prepared one of two ways: uncooked, so you can deep fry or boil them, or lightly fried so they merely need to be reheated. We couldn't get the secret recipe from Tommy Thompson, president and co-owner, but he did tell us how they prepare "Crabmeat Bisque."

The Chesapeake Restaurant has been serving up the Chesapeake Bay's bounty for over seventy-five years. "Crab Imperial Chesapeake," a type of crab casserole, is a specialty. They suggest their cold leek soup, a spinach salad, breadsticks, and lemon chiffon pie, along with a Moselle Reisling wine to compliment the casserole entree. Delicious.

Harvey Marshall, owner and operator of *Captain Harvey's* had Chef Rudolph Speckamp send a recipe for the appetizer known as Captain's Toast, a favorite with their clientele. All three of these restaurants have good service, food, and are reasonably priced.

As we said, crabcakes are served in the press box in Baltimore. One of the nice ladies working there was sweet enough to volunteer her version of Maryland crabcakes for us, so we decided to start the Maryland chapter with her basic crabcakes recipe.

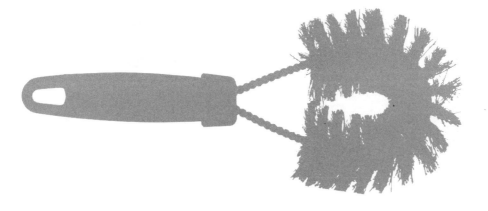

BALTIMORE

CAPTAIN'S TOAST

Captain Harvey's

4 slices white bread, 2½ in. thick
4 doz. mussels
4 shallots
2 cloves garlic
1 cup white wine
1 cup cream
¼ lb. mushrooms, sliced
2 T. butter
dill
salt
pepper
roux (2 T. butter, 2 T. flour)
lemon juice, to taste
Worcestershire sauce, to taste

☐ Deep fry bread and hollow out. In the meantime, take fresh mussels and place in casserole dish with butter, shallots, and garlic on the bottom. Glaze with white wine. Cover and steam until mussels pop open. Remove them from heat. Take mussels out of the shell and strain liquid. In separate pot, add sliced mushrooms and strained liquid and boil two minutes. Remove from heat and add cream. Bind with roux, add dill, salt, white pepper, lemon juice, and Worcestershire sauce. Add mussels and heat through. Adjust seasonings. Place equal amounts over bread slices. Serve immediately. Serves 4.

MARYLAND CRABCAKES

1 lb. lump crabmeat
1½ tsp. salt
1 T. butter, melted
1 tsp. dry mustard
2 tsp. Worcestershire sauce
1 T. parsley, chopped
1 egg yolk
½ tsp. pepper, or to taste
1 T. mayonnaise
½ tsp. paprika
bread crumbs
oil, for frying

☐ Pick over crab for shells. Add all ingredients but crumbs, mixing lightly. Shape in 4 to 6 cakes, roll in crumbs, and sauté lightly in hot fat. Serves 4 to 6.

CRAB IMPERIAL CHESAPEAKE

The Chesapeake Restaurant

1 green pepper, finely chopped
2 pimientos, finely chopped
2 eggs
1 cup mayonnaise
1 T. salt
1 T. English mustard
½ tsp. white pepper
3 lb. lump crabmeat
additional mayonnaise
paprika

☐ In a bowl, combine green pepper, pimiento, eggs, 1 cup mayonnaise, salt, mustard, and pepper; mix well. Add crabmeat and mix gently, being careful not to break up crab pieces. Spoon mixture into 8 crab-shells or individual casseroles, mounding lightly. Spread tops with a thin layer of additional mayonnaise and sprinkle with paprika. Bake at 350°F. for 15–18 minutes. Serve hot, or chill and serve on a bed of lettuce. If desired, garnish with lemon and tomato rose. Makes 8 servings.

Note: To prepare crab shells for stuffing, select large perfect shells and scrub them thoroughly with a wire brush. Place shells in a Dutch oven and cover with hot water. Add 1 teaspoon of baking soda and bring to a boil. Simmer covered, for about 20 minutes. Then drain, wash, and dry shells. This removes the fishy odor. The shells may be stored and reused. Just simmer again with baking soda after each use.

We found the Baltimore waterfront a pleasant place for a bite and a stroll.

Photo by Jim Conroy

CRAB MEAT BISQUE

Thompson's Sea Girt House

1½ lb. backfin crabmeat
8 oz. Chablis wine
1 T. Spanish paprika
1 qt. clam juice, heated
1 qt. Half & Half, heated
2 tsp. chicken granules (makes bouillon), heated
salt to taste
1½ cup all-purpose flour
1 cup salad oil

☐ Heat salad oil over medium heat, add paprika, and stir with whip for one minute. Add flour gradually while stirring constantly, until all flour is absorbed. Continue stirring for 5 minutes. Then add heated Half & Half gradually. While stirring, add warm clam juice, then stir in wine. Add hot bouillon and crabmeat and continue stirring for 10 more minutes. Let stand 3 minutes and serve. Serves 4 to 6.

BUFFALO

Chicken wings and snow, snow, snow. If you follow the national weather then you know that Buffalo gets more snow than anywhere in the United States. And there are probably more chicken wings eaten in Buffalo than anywhere in the country. We haven't found any correlation, but if you are interested in "what the big deal is with chicken wings," maybe you should ask Dom (The Rooster) Bellismo of *Frank & Theresa's Anchor Bar*. It's said they have the best "wings" in Buffalo. There's a secret to the spices involved. If you want the real thing, he'll be glad to make you some, but the recipe stays at the Anchor Bar. But we did get a terrific recipe for wings from *Mulligan's Cafe & Nightclub*, a good place for both food and entertainment; Chef Carriera shared his recipe.

There are two major ethnic groups in Buffalo, Italian and Polish, so we've included recipes from two restaurants that represent these groups. At *Salvatore's Italian Gardens*, Russel Salvatore, the owner, and his son Joseph go out of their way to make you feel welcome. The de-

cor is also worth noting. This has to be the most ornate restaurant ever built—from the gardens, statues and fountains outside, to the detailed model of Rome inside. Some call it beautiful, some call it gaudy. We promise that whatever you think of it, you'll never forget it.

The Polish Villa was chosen because the "locals" in Cheektowaga (just outside of Buffalo) say it's the best. The restaurant features a buffet that looks like "The History of Polish Food."

If you have time for a ride in the country, you might take the pleasant drive out to the Alabama Swamps. Alabama? Yes, and in New York. The Iroquois National Wildlife Refuge there attracts thousands of Canadian geese, mallards, black ducks, and pintails on their way south along the Atlantic Flyway. Just turn left when you get to the Alabama Hotel. You might stop in there and say hello to the Woodwards. They run the restaurant there, a little place "off the beaten path" that is jam-packed on Sundays for their ham, "Chicken n' Biscuits," and "Grandma's Pies," all served family-style.

In Buffalo, it takes more than 12° and twelve inches of snow to cool Bills fans.

VEAL ROYALE

Salvatore's Italian Gardens

1½ lb. veal scaloppine
3 T. butter
1 large onion, sliced
½ tsp. nutmeg
1 tsp. paprika
½ cup white wine
1 cup sour cream
Salt and Pepper to taste

☐ Melt butter in large saucepan. Add onions and cook until limp (do not brown). Cut veal into 2-inch cubes, add and sear on all sides. Add wine and seasonings. Simmer until the wine is reduced to half. Add sour cream, stir and bring to a slow boil. Serve with rice pilaf or buttered noodles with parsley.

"BUFFALO STYLE" CHICKEN WINGS

Mulligan's Cafe & Nightclub

2 lbs. (12–16) chicken wings
1 cup butter
2 oz. barbecue sauce (see Kansas City)
1 tsp. salt
1 tsp. pepper
2 Tbsp. lemon juice
1 Tbsp.–1½ oz. Tabasco to taste

☐ Deep fry chicken wings. Melt butter in small pan. Add ingredients and bring to low boil. Remove from heat and pour into a bowl with chicken and mix together, coating chicken. Buffalo style is to serve on a plate with bleu cheese dressing and celery on the side. The chicken wings are dipped in the bleu cheese dressing. Serves 6.

MASHED POTATO DUMPLINGS

The Polish Villa

2 cups flour
2 eggs
3 cups mashed potatoes, hot
Salt to taste
water

☐ Mix all above ingredients and add water to achieve desired texture. Drop mixture by teaspoon into salted boiling water. Boil until dumplings float to top. Drain. Serve in soup. Makes 8 servings.

GOLUMBKI
(Cabbage Rolls)

The Polish Villa

1 whole head of cabbage
1½ onion, chopped
2 T. butter
4 bacon strips
¼ loaf bread, absorbed in water, crumbled
1½ lb. ground beef
½ lb. ground fresh pork
1½ cups rice, cooked
1 tsp. salt
¼ tsp. pepper
3 10-oz. cans tomato soup

☐ Cut head of cabbage in half and remove core. Place cabbage in kettle filled with boiling salted water. Cover and cook until cabbage is softened to pull off leaves. Sauté onion and chopped bacon strips in butter. Add to meat, rice, salt, pepper, and crumbled bread. Mix thoroughly. Place a heaping tablespoon of meat mixture on each cabbage leaf. Tuck in sides of leaf while rolling. Place toothpicks in rolls, if desired. Place layers of rolls into roaster. Combine tomato soup with one can of water, and pour over cabbage. Place covered roaster in oven at 350° F., for about 2 hours. Makes 15 servings.

The ornate door of Salvatore's Italian Gardens *insures you'll never forget your visit.*

Sometimes you have to go far north to taste a bit of the South — Alabama in Buffalo.

FETTUCINE ALFREDO

Salvatore's Italian Gardens

1 lb. Fettucine noodles (cooked *al dente*)
3 cups béchamel sauce (made from lightly flavored chicken stock, dash white pepper, nutmeg and garlic)
Add:
1½ cups domestic grated cheese, stirring with wire whip until cheese melts into sauce
Add:
2 cups drawn butter, stirring into sauce and whipping vigorously until butter is completely dissolved

☐ Garnish with chopped fresh parsley and ground black pepper. Serves 4, as entrees, 12, as side dish.

CHICKEN SOUP

The Polish Villa

4 lb. soup chicken, split into 8 pieces
2 qt. water
¼ tsp. pepper
2 carrots
2 celery stalks
1 onion, chopped
2 T. parsley, chopped

☐ Start chicken in cold water, so it does not make water cloudy. Add celery, onion, carrots, pepper, and parsley. Cook soup for about an hour; serve hot or store in refrigerator. Serves 6 to 8.

CHICAGO

Everyone knows Chicago is called the "Windy City" but there is a misconception as to why. If you were to stand in Soldier Field, home of the Chicago Bears, almost anytime, any day, you would say it's the prevailing westerly winds steadily blowing across the flatlands of the Midwest that gave the city its nickname. It actually started back in the 1890s about the time George Ferris invented his wheel for the World's Columbian Exposition. The 36 car "Ferris Wheel" was so large it could accommodate 2160 passengers at once. This set Chicagoans to bragging. They got a little long-winded in their praise, and surrounding farmers took to calling Chicago the "Windy City."

Chicagoans can still find things to brag about. The Chicago Board of Trade is the world's largest commodity exchange. Buckingham Fountain is the world's largest lighted fountain. The Sears Tower is the world's tallest building. Chicago also has approximately 250,000 Greek Americans, probably the largest Greek community in the United States. It's been said there are more Greeks in Chicago than anywhere except Athens.

We chose the *Parthenon* from Greektown, an area along South Halstead Street, to represent the community. It is owned by Chris and Bill Liakouris. For under $8.00, Chef Angelo Gailas makes souvlaki, Greek shishkabob, spanakotiropita (spinach-cheese pie), and baklava for dessert.

Two more restaurants worth bragging about are *Lawry's The Prime Rib* and *Nick's Fishmarket.* Lawry's originally started in Beverly Hills but it seems very much at home in the city that once boasted the largest "stockyards" in the country. The stockyards are gone, but you can still get a perfect prime rib at Lawry's, carved right at the table. Lawry's has only one entree, the standing roast prime rib of beef. The idea, started by Lawrence L. Frank in 1938, broke the traditional concept of a restaurant at that time. His idea of a "tossed salad" before the entree, along with dressing up a baked potato with condiments to make a respectable side dish, are now "traditional" in many American restaurants. (The salad recipe is included under Chicago; the other Lawry's recipes are listed under Los Angeles, home of the original Lawry's).

Nick's Fishmarket, unlike Lawry's, offers some sixty entrees including abalone, mahi-mahi, catfish, snapper, swordfish, as well as a wide selection of veal, chicken and beef dishes. Aside from the delicious food and attentive service we like Nick's for its intimate decor. Oversized private booths are equipped with phone jacks and dimmer switches for the lights; you can "raise the lights" to read the menu, and then lower them for a more romantic setting. There is also a lounge for dancing and relaxing. Say hello to Bobby the bartender for us when you stop in.

Pizzeria #Uno in downtown Chicago may have the best pizza in the Midwest, some think in the U.S. (but you know about Chicagoans and their bragging). Uno's has a secret recipe. Part of the secret is cornmeal in the dough. Mrs. Frances Woolf from Uno's promises this recipe is as close as they'll let you come to the secret, and hey, it makes a great pizza. Along with Pizzeria #Uno is *Pizzeria Due* right around the corner. Same pizza, just another great place to order it. You can also buy these pizzas frozen and packaged to go. We've brought them back for friends in New York by plane. You may have a problem, though, keeping the flight attendants from putting the pizza in the plane's microwave oven en route home!

Next to Uno's is a Mexican restaurant that serves good food, called *Su Casa.* It's also owned by the folks at Uno's. They were nice enough to send a few recipes from there as well.

Jim Heneghan, resident pizza expert, thinks he may have discovered the secret to Uno's crust.

Photo by ABC Sports

DEEP-DISH PIZZA, CHICAGO STYLE

Pizzeria #Uno

Crust

¼ cup shortening
1½ T. sugar
1 tsp. salt
1½ packages active dry yeast
¾ cup yellow cornmeal
3–3½ cups all-purpose flour
olive oil

☐   Heat 1 cup water, shortening, sugar, and salt un-til shortening melts; cool to lukewarm. Soften yeast in ½ cup lukewarm water. Combine yeast and shorten-ing mixtures in large bowl. Add cornmeal. Add 2 cups flour; beat well. Stir in enough additional flour to make a soft dough. Turn onto lightly floured board; knead until smooth and elastic, working in more flour as needed. Brush a round 12- or 14-in. pizza pan (at least 2 inches deep) with oil and sprinkle lightly with corn-meal. Press dough evenly over bottom and up sides of pan. Bake at 425° F. for 7 minutes. Set aside.

Filling

1 lb. pork sausage meat
1 12-oz. can peeled, crushed plum tomatoes
1 tsp. dried basil
1 tsp. oregano
olive oil
12 oz. mozzarella cheese, thinly sliced
½ cup Parmesan cheese, grated

☐   Cook pork sausage meat over medium heat. Re-move from heat and drain off excess fat. Mix basil and oregano into tomatoes. Drizzle small amount of olive oil over partially cooked crust. Arrange mozzarella slices all over crust. Crumble cooked pork sausage meat over cheese. Top with tomato mixture, sprinkle with Parmesan cheese. Bake at 425° F. for 45 minutes or until crust is golden brown. Let stand 5 minutes before serving.

Note: This recipe has been tested on numerous occasions, thanks to one of our hand-held camera-men, Jim Heneghan, a pizza lover from way back. He says if you experiment a bit using portions of both regular flour and self-rising flour for the 3 cups of flour (i.e., 2 cups all-purpose and 1 self-rising, or 1½ cups each) you can come pretty close to the secret recipe.

SALAD BOWL À LA LAWRY'S

Lawry's The Prime Rib

1 small head Romaine
1 small head iceberg lettuce
½ cup watercress, torn in sprigs
1 cup shoestring beets, well-drained
1 egg, hard cooked and sieved
Lawry's seasoned salt
Lawry's seasoned pepper
¾ cup Lawry's Famous French Dressing
6 cherry tomatoes

☐   Tear romaine and lettuce into pieces. Add water-cress, beets and eggs. Sprinkle with Seasoned Salt and Seasoned Pepper. Toss with Famous French Dressing. Place 1 cherry tomato on each plate with serving of salad. Serves 6.

CHILE RELLENO
(Stuffed Pepper)

Su Casa

Peppers
6 bell peppers
1 lb. Monterey cream cheese
3 eggs
oil and vinegar

☐ Broil peppers evenly. Remove from oven, place in paper bag, close tightly. Allow to steam in closed bag for approximately 20 minutes. Remove from bag, peel outer skin. Cut ½ inch from stem end of pepper, remove seeds with spoon. Marinate peppers overnight in equal parts of oil and vinegar.

Next day: Drain and stuff with Monterey cream cheese. Separate eggs. Beat whites until stiff, fold in slightly beaten egg yolks. Roll peppers in flour, dip in egg mixture one at a time. Drop in deep frying pan with enough hot oil to cover. Brown evenly, remove and drain.

Sauce
1 onion, thinly sliced
3 T. olive oil
1 clove garlic
3½ cups chicken stock
½ cup white wine
3 No. 303 cans solid pack tomatoes (6 cups)
1 tsp. oregano
1 bay leaf
3 tsp. salt
1 tsp. pepper

☐ Fry onion and garlic in olive oil until onion becomes transparent. Strain tomatoes through sieve, combine with onion and garlic, add chicken stock and wine. Add seasoning. Bring to boil, simmer for few minutes. Correct seasoning if desired.

Twenty minutes before serving place peppers in sauce and simmer until thoroughly heated.

FLAN

Su Casa

1½ cups sugar
5 cups milk
2 cinnamon sticks
¼ tsp. salt
1 tsp. vanilla

☐ Heat 1 cup sugar in heavy saucepan until dark brown caramel syrup is formed. Pour syrup in bottom of six custard cups. Scald milk with cinnamon sticks. Beat eggs lightly. Add ½ cup sugar, salt, vanilla, and milk, a little at a time. Mix thoroughly. Pour in custard cups on top of caramel. Set custard cups in pan of hot water and bake at 325° F. for 1 hour or until knife inserted in center comes out clean. Serves 6.

SPANAKOTIROPITA
(Spinach-Cheese Pie)

Parthenon

2 10-oz. packages frozen spinach, chopped
½ cup green onion, minced
½ cup white onion, minced
2 T. butter
½ cup heavy cream
1 T. salt
1 tsp. pepper
6 eggs
12 oz. feta cheese
½ cup dill, chopped
1 lb. fillo leaves (paper-thin pastry dough)
1 cup butter, melted

☐ Defrost spinach and drain well. Sauté the minced green and white onions in butter. Add spinach, stir well and cook about 7 minutes. Stir in cream, salt, and pepper. Cook for about 5 more minutes. Remove from heat. Beat eggs, add to mixture, and mix well. Add crumbled feta cheese and chopped dill. Stir thoroughly.

Use an 8 x 8 x 1½-inch pan. Line the bottom with half the fillo sheets, brushing each generously with butter. Spread the filling over the fillo and cover with remaining fillo, brushing each layer with butter. Pour any remaining butter over top. Score through the top layers of fillo in size pieces desired. Bake at 350° F. for 1 hour. Makes 12 large or 20 small pieces.

BAKLAVA
(Honey Nut Pastry)

Parthenon

1 lb. fillo leaves
1 lb. butter, melted
2½ lb. honey
2 lb. walnuts, chopped
ground cloves and cinnamon

☐ Butter shallow baking pan. Cover bottom with 1 layer of fillo, turning edges under to fit pan. Brush fillo with butter, repeat 4 layers. Butter fourth layer and spread with a handful of chopped nuts, sprinkled with spices. Crumble slightly the next layer of fillo to relieve heaviness of too many layers of fillo. (This should be done to about every third layer.) Butter each layer of fillo and cover with nuts and spices, repeating this process until about 4 sheets of fillo remain. Brush remaining 4 layers with butter only, but do not butter top layer. Cut contents diagonally in desired size with sharp knife. Bake in 350° F. oven 45 to 55 minutes, until golden brown. Take from oven, pour honey over immediately. Cool. Cover with waxed paper and let stand 24 hours.

They call him "Sweetness," but Walter Payton might be more aptly named "Toughness."

PASTICHIO
(Pasta and Meat Sauce with Béchamel)

Parthenon

Meat sauce
1 T. butter
1 onion, grated
1 lb. lean ground beef
1 tsp. salt
¼ tsp. pepper
¼ tsp. nutmeg
½ cup dry white wine
¼ cup tomato sauce
½ cup boiling water
¼ cup kefalotyri cheese, grated (or Parmesan)

Pasta
½ lb. macaroni in whole long pieces
3 qt. boiling water
1 T. salt
¼ cup butter
2 eggs, slightly beaten
½ cup kefalotyri cheese, grated (or Parmesan)

Béchamel sauce
¼ cup butter
1 T. flour
4 cups milk
1 tsp. salt
¼ tsp. nutmeg
3 whole eggs plus 3 yolks
¼ cup kefalotyri cheese, grated (or Parmesan)

Topping
1 cup kefalotyri cheese, grated (or Parmesan)

☐ In a heavy skillet melt the butter, sauté the onion a few minutes, then add meat. Break up the meat with a fork as it browns so there are no lumps. Drain off the fat, then add salt, pepper, nutmeg, and wine. Cover and simmer 5 minutes. Mix tomato sauce with boiling water and add to skillet. Cover and simmer 45 minutes. Remove from flame, stir in cheese, and mix well. Set aside.

Break macaroni sticks in half and add to boiling water with salt. Boil for 15 or 18 minutes. Pour out the water, fill pan with scalding water to wash away starch, then pour macaroni into colander to drain. Melt butter in the same pan, return the drained macaroni and stir to mix butter through it. Add the slightly beaten eggs and cheese and stir until well mixed. Set aside.

Melt butter for béchamel cream sauce in a saucepan. Make flour into a paste by adding a little of the milk. Then add flour paste, milk, salt, and nutmeg to saucepan. Heat, stirring constantly, until milk comes to a boil, then remove from heat. Beat eggs and yolks well and add to cream sauce, beating to keep smooth. Add cheese and beat again until smooth.

Use a buttered 8 x 8 x 2-in. pan (must be at least this deep), and assemble layers as follows: half the macaroni, ¼ cup grated cheese, all the meat sauce, 4 tablespoons cream sauce, balance of macaroni, ¼ cup grated cheese, balance of cream sauce, and balance of grated cheese.

Bake at 350° F. for 40 minutes or until knife inserted in center comes out clean. Let stand in a warm place, uncovered, for 2 hours to become firmly set. Return to warm oven for a few minutes before serving. Serves 8 to 10.

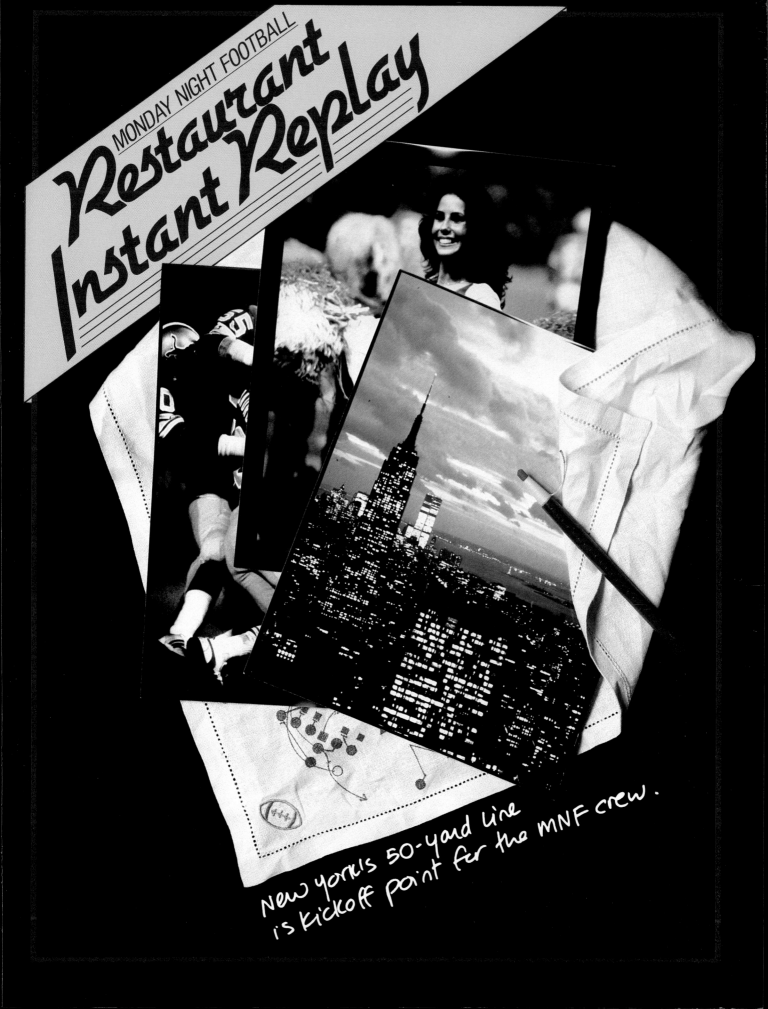

Instant Replay

Not even a Saints game tops a ride through the French Quarter.

That superb luau at Coco Palms made the frenetic Pro Bowl bearable.

A spectacular half-time at the Pro Bowl.

Only a stone's throw from Cleveland Stadium... the best "Shrimp Scampi" in the midwest.

Instant Replay

An incredible breakfast at the Eggshell fortified us well for a day in the glorious Rockies.

The view's great from up here, but the food's all down there.

When you're driving around Buffalo and suddenly think you've found Venice... turn in for Salvatore's fantastic fettucine.

must include
Zabar's
Reuben and
antipasto if I
ever do write
that Monday
Night Football
Cookbook...

The most
memorable
pass of
Green Bay's
season.

I promised Debra Boston's finest stuffed sole. the next time we're in town.

It's hard work being a cameraman, with all that equipment to lug around.

Instant Replay

I Can't eat all the time...

"America's Team" squeaked into the '81 playoffs... and were beaten by the upstart 49ers. But the Cowboys always come back.

GAZPACHO

Nick's Fishmarket

8 ripe tomatoes, peeled and diced
1 large green pepper, seeded, and diced
2 cucumbers, peeled, seeded, and diced
1 large sweet onion, diced (set aside ¼ portion)
1½ cloves garlic, minced
2 T. olive oil
3 T. Worcestershire sauce
6 drops Tabasco sauce (or more, to taste)
2 tsp. salt
½ tsp. pepper
24 oz. tomato juice
vodka

☐ Combine all ingredients except ¼ portion of diced onion and chill the mixture overnight, or 2–3 days ahead of time, in a covered bowl. Ladle into soup bowls and splash with vodka before serving. As garnishes, set out: croutons, chopped hard-boiled egg, and diced onion. Serves 10–12.

AVGOLEMONO SOUPA
(Egg-Lemon Soup)

Parthenon

6 cups chicken stock
½ cup rice
1 tsp. flour
¼ cup water
3 eggs
juice of 2 lemons

☐ Bring the stock to a boil and add salt and rice. Cover and boil gently 18 minutes. Measure out 3 cups of the stock into a small saucepan. Cover the remaining stock and rice and keep hot. Make a paste of the flour and water, add to the 3 cups of stock and boil gently for 5 minutes. In a large bowl, beat the eggs with an electric beater until thick and light in color. Continue to beat while alternately adding, by the spoonful, the 3 cups of stock and lemon juice. Continue beating a few minutes then stir into hot rice soup, blending thoroughly. Serves 4–6.

SOUVLAKI
(Shishkebab)

Parthenon

2–3 lb. leg of lamb or pork tenderloin
3 T. salt
1 T. pepper
2 T. oregano
¼ cup olive oil
juice of half lemon
1 tomato, large
½ onion
1 green pepper
1 cup wine

☐ Clean and trim meat. Cut into 2-inch cubes. Put cubes in a large bowl and season with salt, pepper, and oregano. Toss with olive oil, lemon juice, and wine, mixing well. Refrigerate mixture for approximately 2 hours.

Cut tomato in eight pieces. Cut onion and green pepper in 4 pieces each. Skewer meat and vegetables for each of four servings. To skewer, begin with one cube meat, then alternate meat with one piece each of tomato, onion, green pepper, tomato, and ending with one cube meat. Place skewers approximately 6 inches from flame. Cook to desired doneness, turning occasionally. Serves 4.

NICK'S SEAFOOD BENEDICT

Nick's Fishmarket

Each serving consists of:
½ lightly toasted English muffin
1 helping of seafood in béchamel sauce
1 poached egg
hollandaise sauce

To prepare the uncooked seafood, bring to a boil:
3 cups water
1 cup dry white wine
1 bay leaf

Add, for 2–3 minutes or until tender:
1½ lb. bay scallops
1½ lb. shrimp
1 lb. mushrooms, sliced (1 minute only)

Drain and remove bay leaf. Set aside.
Prepare béchamel sauce by slowly heating:
8 T. butter

Then slowly stir in:
8 T. flour
4 cups milk

☐ Add a pinch each of nutmeg, salt, pepper and thyme to taste. Continue to cook over low heat for 3–5 minutes, until it thickens. Then combine sauce with poached seafood and mushrooms. Cover to keep warm. Serve with a broiled tomato; serves 12.

Prepare hollandaise sauce:
1 cup butter
6 egg yolks
4 T. lemon juice
½ tsp. salt
pinch cayenne

☐ Heat butter to bubbling; do not brown. Put other ingredients in a blender, cover and turn on low speed. Remove cover while machine is still operating and slowly add hot butter. When all butter is added, turn off machine and serve. (Sauce may be reheated by placing it in a small pot resting in 2 inches of hot water in a large saucepan. To thin, add 1 tablespoon hot water. To thicken, heat water in saucepan to boiling and continue to stir Hollandaise in small pot.)

CINCINNATI

In 1788, settlers from the Middle Atlantic states purchased a million acres of land along the Ohio River. The major settlement there was named after the Society of Cincinnati, an organization of Revolutionary officers who were named to honor the Roman hero Lucius Quintius Cincinnatus. The settlement grew to become a manufacturing and trading center of the Midwest. It became a gateway to the South as steamboats traveling the Ohio brought people and goods to and from the southern states. These days, Riverfront Stadium, home of the 1981 AFC Champion Bengals, stands tall on the shoreline, and the *Delta Queen,* a Cincinnati riverboat, cruises down to Louisville the week before the Kentucky Derby for a race against the *Belle of Louisville,* another "sternwheeler." There is never much of a contest as the engines of the *Belle* are not as powerful as the *Delta Queen's* but a good time is always had by those both on board and on the shore.

A place for good times in Cincinnati is *Rookwood Pottery.* It sits atop Mount Adams, an area northeast of downtown that seems to stand at an angle. If you live near Cincinnati and wonder what it's like to walk up and down the famous hills of San Francisco, Mount Adams is the place to visit. There are many shops, bars and restaurants on the way up. Rookwood Pottery is at the top. Inside is the clever renovation of a round-roomed brick structure that was once a pottery mill. It is now a busy place for eating, drinking and meeting people.

A new addition to the downtown area is *R. Tapley's.* It's a bi-level space done in contemporary art deco. Veal is the specialty, and Patrick Gaito, the chef, sent us "Veal St. Moritz," as well as recipes for hollandaise and béarnaise sauces to top off the dish.

Two restaurants we highly recommend are *Maisonette* and *La Normandie.* Maisonette has been named a top restaurant in the United States by many different sources. Both restaurants are operated by the same management, and both are for special occasions when the dining experience is the major event of the evening.

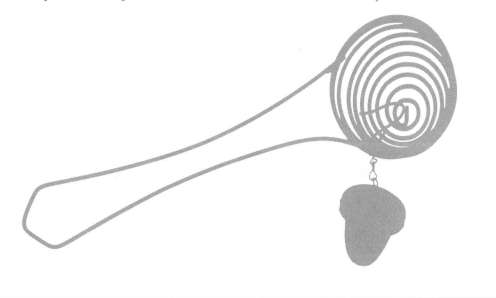

Music Hall.

SHRIMP "MAISONETTE"

Maisonette

1½ lb. shrimp, frozen, peeled, and deveined (4 oz.
    per person)
2 shallots, finely chopped
4 cloves fresh garlic, chopped
¼ lb. butter
½ lb. fresh mushrooms, sliced
1 cup Chablis wine
2 T. parsley, chopped
juice of ½ lemon
salt and pepper

☐ Cook the shrimp as directed on package. Split lengthwise and put aside. Preheat frying pan and melt butter. Add shallots (if not available, use onion) and cook for about 30 seconds until transparent but not brown. Add chopped garlic and mushrooms. Cook 30 seconds, mixing well at all times.

Add the sliced shrimp and cook for about 30 seconds. Add Chablis and cook for 2 minutes. Add chopped parsley and salt and pepper to taste. Squeeze half lemon directly over shrimp, mix well and serve immediately in a rice ring or over a slice of fresh toast. The dish may be used as an appetizer or main course, and is greatly enhanced by serving with a good dry Chablis. Serves 6.

BÉARNAISE SAUCE

R. Tapley's

2 T. tarragon vinegar
2 tsp. fresh tarragon or 1 tsp. dried
6 shallots, minced
1 T. dry white wine
4 egg yolks
¼ tsp. salt
¼ tsp. mustard
⅛ tsp. meat glaze (Bovil)
⅛ tsp. Escoffier's Sauce Robert

☐ In a small pan, heat tarragon vinegar, tarragon, shallots, and wine and simmer until almost all liquid is absorbed. Place mixture in blender, add egg yolks, salt, mustard, meat glaze, and Sauce Robert. Blend for 15 seconds.

Heat butter until sizzling hot. Pour butter in a steady stream into the running blender. Blend until thick.

HOLLANDAISE SAUCE

R. Tapley's

3 egg yolks
½ cup butter (1 stick)
1 T. lemon juice
pinch of salt

☐ Warm the container of a food processor by filling it with very hot water and leaving it to stand for 2–3 minutes, then drain and dry it. Break in the egg yolks and add salt. Turn on the processor, heat the butter in a small pan until bubbling, add the lemon juice and pour the mixture slowly through the hole in the lid of the processor. As soon as all the butter is amalgamated, switch off. Spoon into a warm sauce boat and serve immediately, or if it must be kept for a few minutes, stand it over a pan of very hot water. *Note: do not reheat the sauce.*

VEAL ST. MORITZ

R. Tapley's

6 oz. veal cutlet (per person)
½ cup shallots, minced
½ lb. fresh mushrooms
butter
white wine

☐ Start with a 6-ounce veal cutlet (use only the finest white, milk-fed veal). Cut a pocket in the veal and stuff with minced shallots and sliced fresh mushrooms that have been sautéed in butter.

Dust the cutlet in seasoned flour and sauté in butter and white wine. Immediately top half of the cutlet with hollandaise sauce and the other half with béarnaise sauce.

CHOCOLATE PROFITEROLE

La Normandie

Paté à Chou (Chou Paste)

3 cups water
¾ cups butter, melted
3 cups flour, sifted
½ tsp. salt
12 or 14 eggs, medium

☐ In a saucepan, place water, butter, and salt. Bring to a boil, then add sifted flour all at once. Stir well on the fire for a few minutes until the paste is dry and doesn't cling to the pan or wooden spoon. Take off fire, let cool a few minutes, then add eggs one by one, stirring each egg into the paste.

Put mixture in a pastry bag, and pipe 1-inch balls on baking sheet.

Bake in a 375° F. oven for approximately 20 minutes. Let cool.

Cut in half horizontally. Fill with a scoop of chocolate ice cream. Spoon rum sauce on top. Add a touch of chocolate syrup to garnish. Serves 6.

Pastry Cream for Rum Sauce

½ lb. powdered sugar
2 oz. cornstarch
6 egg yolks
½ qt. boiling milk
½ pt. whipping cream
6 oz. dark rum

☐ Mix first four ingredients and cook, stirring constantly. Remove after the first boil. Change container and cool on ice. When cold, add lightly whipped cream and dark rum. Strain through a fine strainer to eliminate all the lumps.

Delta Queen, *a Cincinnati riverboat, cruises down to Louisville every year for its own pre-Derby race.*

CLEVELAND

General Moses Cleveland, the pioneer surveyor of northern Ohio, founded the city in 1796. It grew commercially when water routes to the Ohio River and along the Great Lakes were opened. Ohio's largest city is known for its steel, tool, and shipping industries. Cleveland can boast of one of the country's first professional theaters, a world-renowned symphony orchestra and the Cleveland Museum of Art's fine collection.

Most of our time here is spent in the Cleveland Stadium. Most of the paintings we've seen are on people's faces in the endzone stands. In Cleveland, fan is short for fanatic. A place you'll find many fans from both the stadium and the music hall is *Pat Joyce's Tavern on the Mall*. You may find some players there as well, perusing the menu that features steaks, seafood, and prime ribs.

Within walking distance of the stadium are a number of fine places. *John Q's Public Bar & Grille* and *The Whole Grain* are run by the same company and happen to be next door to one another. The Whole Grain is open for breakfast and lunch, specializing in soups, gumbos, and chowders featured daily from their list of over forty. There are also salads, sandwiches, and desserts. Catering to the workweek lunch crowd, it is closed on weekends.

John Q's serves lunch and dinner every day except Sunday. The fare is seafood, steak, and prime rib for dinner; sandwiches, burgers, quiches, and omelettes are on the lunch menu. Specialties of the house include "Chinese Chicken with Stir Fry Vegetables" and a "Shrimp and Scallops Sauté." The decor is a combination of modern and turn of the century. One of our co-workers would call it a "fern bar," meaning there is a hand-carved bar, brass railings, mirrors, healthy ferns and potted plants. Velvet curtained booths can make for an intimate dinner. Reservations are requested, and a must if you'd like a booth.

Captain Frank's seafood house is next to the stadium as well. Featuring fish from fresh water as well as from the sea, it sits at the end of a wharf on the shore of Lake Erie. Captain Frank is known as the man who brought "scampi" to the Midwest. According to the Captain, many places that advertise "Scampi" are serving only "plain ol' shrimp." The only way to find out if what he claims is true, is to order "Scampi" and see the difference. The place is not fancy; it's the food that has made Captain Frank's reputation. Monday Night Football fans will be pleased that it stays open late at night. If you're in a hurry, there is a takeout counter at the rear.

The Pewter Mug is a posh pub downtown in the Citizens Building featuring "eye of rib" steaks, great burgers, and an outstanding dish called "Honey Dipped Chicken." Reservations are a must here.

At Captain Frank's, *you can sample shrimp from the man who brought "scampi" to the Midwest.*

Photo by the author

CHINESE CHICKEN WITH STIR-FRY VEGETABLES

John Q's Public Bar and Grille

1 lb., 2 oz. boneless chicken breasts, skin removed, cut in strips 1 in. by 2 in.
3¾ oz. zucchini
2¼ oz. broccoli
2¼ oz. mushrooms
3¾ oz. celery
2¼ oz. fresh pea pods
2¼ oz. fresh bean sprouts
3 T. oil, for frying
3 T. Teriyake Marinade (pork sauté)
⅛ tsp. ground ginger

☐ Prepare each vegetable. Scrub and wash zucchini, cut in 2½ in. lengths. Wash broccoli: cut stem cuds *only,* crosswise in ¼ in. slices. Slice mushrooms lengthwise, caps and stems, ¼ in. thick. Wash celery, slice crosswise into ½ in. slices. Wash and pat dry bean sprouts with paper towel, then do same with pea pods.

Marinate chicken in Teriyake from 30 minutes to 12 hours. Place wok (or frying pan) over medium flame for 30 seconds. Add 1 tablespoon of oil, and heat for 20 seconds or until oil is hot but not smoking. Add ginger and stir fry for 15 seconds. Add broccoli, zucchini, and celery and stir fry for 1 minute. Turn flame to high. Add pea pods, sprouts, and mushrooms and stir fry for one minute. Empty contents of wok into a heated serving dish. Do *not* wash wok. Stir marinated chicken with chopsticks. Heat remaining 2 tablespoons of oil in the same wok. Add chicken and stir fry about 2 minutes. Remove from the wok. Restir seasoning sauce and add along with vegetables and stir fry one more minute or until thoroughly mixed and hot. Empty contents of wok into heated serving dish. Serve immediately.

SHRIMP AND SCALLOPS SAUTÉ

John Q's & Whole Grain

2½ oz. sea scallops
¼ tsp. salt
2½ oz. shrimp, peeled and deveined cut in half
    lengthwise
1 T. garlic butter
1 T. Chablis wine
2 oz. mushrooms, sautéed in Chablis, drained
3 oz. fresh, whole mushrooms
¼ tsp. salt
1½ tsp. butter
1 T. Chablis wine

☐ Rinse thawed scallops under cold running water and drain well. Cut only the large scallops (approximately 2-in. pieces) in half. Blot dry to remove excess moisture. Scallops must be dry to cook properly. Sprinkle the scallops evenly with salt. Weigh into 2½-ounce portions; cover and refrigerate until needed.

If mushrooms are larger than 1½ in. diameter, cut in halves or quarters. Sprinkle with salt and boil for 3 to 3½ minutes. Drain. Heat butter in a heavy skillet over medium heat until it bubbles. Sauté drained mushrooms 2–3 minutes until tender and slightly browned. Add Chablis and cook 1–2 minutes longer. Keep hot for combining.
Broil immediately before serving:

Melt garlic butter in 7-in. skillet. Add prepared scallops. Stir with a spatula to coat scallops evenly, being careful not to break them. Add Chablis. Cook under a low broiler with the rack on the third notch down, approximately ½ minute. Add shrimp and continue cooking, stirring occasionally to cook evenly, approximately 3 minutes longer. Add sautéed mushrooms in Chablis, stir gently to combine. To serve: place ⅔ cup seasoned rice in skillet near base of handle. Place shrimp-scallop mixture beside rice. Sprinkle mixture with paprika. Garnish skillet at base of handle with lemon crown dipped in paprika on a parsley bouquet.

HONEY-DIPPED CHICKEN

The Pewter Mug

☐ Take a breaded chicken that has been cut into quarters. Deep fry until three-quarters cooked. Take out and coat heavily with honey. Bake at 355° F for approximately seven minutes.

Cleveland and San Diego tangled in the 1981 Monday Night Football *season opener.*

Photo by ABC Sports

DALLAS

The State Fair Park in Dallas is the home of the Hall of Heroes, a memorial to Steven Austin, William Travis, Sam Houston and others who brought pride to the Lone Star State. Exhibits depict the colorful history of Texas, the defense of the Alamo, and Texan independence from Mexico in 1836.

Texas Stadium, home of the Dallas Cowboys, is a modern day hall of heroes. Inside, the great ones who defended the Lone Star here are honored on the wall of the stadium—Chuck Howley, Mel Renfro, Don Perkins, Bob Lilly, and Don Meredith. "Dandy Don" is a native son of Texas, and the state, along with Jeff and Hazel, is very proud of their son.

In the stadium, unlike the Alamo, the home team is usually the favorite. Over the years we have been here many times because the Cowboys are usually a team to watch. This has given us the chance to make friends with some very hospitable Texans.

Pete Dominguez, owner of the *Casa Dominguez* family of restaurants, started making delicious Mexican food for folks down in Austin. Before long he opened more establishments in Dallas and Houston. A visit to one of Pete's places for us is a guarantee of good food, good times and, most important, good friends. (Some of his recipes can also be found under Houston.)

"Totsy" Ianni has been a friend for many years as well, and she and her family run *Ianni's Italian Restaurant*. Dinner on Sunday for us there is like visiting family. After dinner much time is spent talking over coffee or espresso with Sambuca.

A chapter on Texas cuisine would be incomplete without a chicken fried steak. Folks say one of the best is at the *Blackeye Pea*. We're inclined to agree. Gene Street, the owner, sent a broccoli soup recipe to try with it, too.

There are many times when it is impossible to leave for a meal and return to the stadium because of game day traffic. This is when our unit managers, the people who make arrangements and pay the bills for us, must engage the services of a caterer. *Bagelstein's, Inc.* is such an outstanding catering service we just had to give them a mention. Would you believe real New York deli food in the Lone Star state? Larry and Susan Goldstein have got it covered all the way to Dr. Brown's Cel-Ray Tonic, and, oh yes, bagels. They helped us with two good things to spread on bagels along with a deli standard— what else?—Chopped liver.

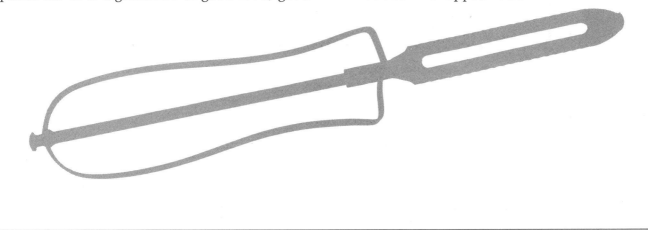

Like football, rodeos, and ten-gallon hats, the Dallas Cowboys Cheerleaders are a Texas institution.

RAISIN CREAM CHEESE

Bagelstein's, Inc.

1 lb. cream cheese
5 oz. raisins
4 T. cinnamon
¼ cup sugar
½ cup walnuts, chopped (optional)

☐ Add raisins to 2 quarts boiling water, stir, reduce heat and simmer 20 minutes. Refrigerate raisins and water until cold. Drain, reserving liquid. Whip cream cheese until smooth. Add drained raisins. Mix. Add cinnamon and sugar slowly. For a thinner consistency add 1 tablespoon of the liquid from the raisins. Optional: add chopped walnuts.

BREAST OF CHICKEN IANNI

Ianni's Italian Restaurant

1 qt. milk
2 tsp. chicken stock
4 oz. melted butter
4 T. flour
1 cup mushrooms
1 T. parsley, chopped
4 boneless chicken breasts

☐ Heat milk. Mix butter, flour, chicken stock, add to heated milk. Stir until thickened; add mushrooms, parsley and stir. Bake chicken at 400° F for about 25 minutes. Pour sauce over chicken. Sprinkle with parsley, if desired. Serves 2 to 4.

VEGETABLE CREAM CHEESE

Bagelstein's, Inc.

¼ lb. green onions (2–3 onions, tops and bottoms, cleaned)
¼ lb. radishes (approx. 10, leave some peel on for color)
1 cucumber, peeled
1½ lb. cream cheese

☐ Whip cream cheese until smooth. Chop vegetables into small pieces, about ½ inch in diameter. Mix vegetables into cheese. A few teaspoons of water may be added to thin mixture to dipping consistency.

Vegetable cream cheese is great spread on a bagel or as a dip for vegetables.

TACOS AL CARBON

Pete Dominguez Restaurants

3 lb. beef skirt steak, marinated overnight
12–15 flour tortillas

Marinade
1 gal. water
1 T. salt
1 bunch cilantro
3 tsp. black pepper
1 T. ground cumin
1 tsp. Tabasco sauce
2 tsp. Worcestershire sauce
dash garlic powder

☐ Broil steak over charcoal grill. Charcoal to desired taste. Slice meat into ½-inch cubes and put in flour tortilla. Roll tortilla and serve. Makes 12–15 Tacos.

CARNE ASADA

Pete Dominguez Restaurants

1 lb. 4 oz. top sirloin steak
2 T. vegetable oil
½ tsp. dried leaf oregano, crushed
½ tsp. salt
¼ tsp. pepper, coarsely ground
¼ cup orange juice
1 T. lime juice
2 tsp. cider vinegar

☐ Place steak in a shallow glass baking dish. Rub oil on each side of steak. Sprinkle with oregano, salt, and pepper. Sprinkle orange juice, lime juice, and vinegar over steak. Cover and refrigerate overnight for best flavor or several hours, turning occasionally.

To cook, bring meat to room temperature. Prepare and pre-heat charcoal grill. Drain meat, reserving marinade. Place steaks on grill over hot coals. Top with orange slices. Occasionally spoon reserved marinade over steaks as they cook. Grill 3–4 minutes on each side, or until medium-rare. Makes 4 servings.

CHICKEN FRIED STEAK BREADING

Blackeye Pea

3 cups flour
1 tsp. salt
1 tsp. fine black pepper
pure vegetable cooking oil

☐ Blend all ingredients. Preheat one inch of pure vegetable cooking oil in heavy skillet, 350° F approximately. Dip cutlet in flour mixture, making sure it is completely covered. Dip cutlet in batter (see accompanying recipe); be sure entire surface is covered. Return cutlet to flour mixture, cover top with mixture and gently press with the heel of your hand. This will make the batter and breading adhere, as well as enlarge the cutlet. Cook for 3 minutes on first side, turn, cook for 3 minutes on the other side, turn again for 1 minute. Hold on a draining rack in warm oven. Repeat this procedure for each cutlet.

Note: The Blackeye Pea uses cutlets cut from choice top round to insure a flavorful and tender steak.

CHICKEN FRIED STEAK BATTER

Blackeye Pea

1 qt. buttermilk
2 eggs
2 T. chicken stock
2 T. MSG
1 tsp. dry mustard
pinch salt
pinch fine black pepper

☐ Beat eggs into buttermilk. Slowly mix in remaining ingredients. Refrigerate. Makes enough batter for six 4-oz. chicken fried steaks.

Photo by ABC Sports

Coach Tom Landry: If you could get under his hat, you might find the secret to building a football dynasty.

Stop in at Casa Dominguez *for some Mexican food — you may be serenaded by Dandy Don on the guitar.*

Photo by the author

SPAGHETTI CARBONARO

Ianni's Italian Restaurant

1 cup onions, chopped
4 eggs
½ lb. crisp bacon, chopped
½ cup Parmesan cheese
1 lb. spaghetti

☐ Cook pasta. Sauté onions in bacon drippings. Pour off grease, add bacon, pasta, cheese, eggs and stir over low heat until blended well. Serves 4.

VEAL PICANTE

Ianni's Italian Restaurant

12 thin slices veal
8 oz. butter, melted
6 cups chicken broth
juice from 3 lemons
2 cups sauterne or white wine
1 T. parsley
1 cup mushrooms
2 T. margarine
flour, to coat veal

☐ Lightly coat veal with flour and sauté in margarine. Drain and add remaining ingredients. Cook about 15 minutes, bringing to a boil and thicken slightly. Serves 4.

CHEESE BROCCOLI SOUP

Blackeye Pea

1½ qt. water
1 8-oz. package frozen broccoli, chopped
1 lb. Velveeta cheese
1 tsp. salt
½ tsp. granulated garlic
pinch black pepper
½ cup cornstarch
1 qt. cold milk

☐ In double boiler, place all ingredients *except* milk and cornstarch. (The cheese will melt faster if broken into pieces.) Cook until cheese is melted. In small container, mix cold milk and cornstarch, making sure there are no lumps. Slowly add the cold milk and cornstarch to the hot cheese-broccoli mixture, and stir to thicken soup. If too thick, add water.

CHEESE NACHOS

Pete Dominguez Restaurants

fried tortilla chips
8 oz. Monterey or cheddar cheese, shredded
½ cup fresh or canned chiles, sliced

☐ Preheat broiler. Top each tortilla chip with mound of cheese and some chile slices. Place on a baking sheet and broil until cheese is just melted. Serve at once. Makes about 48 nachos.

SHRIMP MARINARA

Ianni's Italian Restaurant

4 #16 cans whole tomatoes
8 cloves garlic, chopped
2 T. salt
4 T. sweet basil
2 T. oregano
pinch crushed red pepper
½ cup olive oil
1 cup mushrooms
1½ lb. shrimp

☐ Put first six ingredients in Dutch oven, bring to a boil and simmer 45 minutes, stirring periodically. Add ¼ cup of olive oil and mushrooms and cook 15 minutes more. Sauté shrimp in remaining oil until done. Add shrimp to sauce and serve. May be served with a side dish of pasta. Recipe will make enough sauce for spaghetti. Serves 4.

CHOPPED LIVER

Bagelstein's, Inc.

1 lb. beef liver
1 lb. chicken liver
6 eggs, hard boiled
2 onions, sliced
½ cup vegetable oil
salt
pepper

☐ Wash and drain liver. Boil livers together until done. Put 1 onion through grinder, let drain. (If you don't have a grinder, chop fine in a wooden mixing bowl.) Sauté the other onion in oil for 10 minutes. Stir frequently. Combine cooked liver with the sautéed onion and oil. Put in grinder together with the eggs. Add raw onion and grind again. Add salt and pepper to taste.

Serve as an hors d'oeuvre, or as an appetizer on a bed of lettuce leaves.

This is not Bob Uecker's relative.

DENVER

Denver, known as the "Mile High City" because of its elevation, is situated at the western edge of the Great Plains. The city blossomed during the gold rush of 1859. This was the last place for supplies before setting off west into the mountains, in search of one's fortune. The state capital dome was covered with gold leaf in 1912, in tribute to Colorado miners.

People still go up into the mountains, but they're more likely to be skiing, camping, hang gliding or mountain climbing than gold digging. Few restaurants in Denver strictly enforce a dress code because the outdoor life has made the style more casual. The outdoor life requires a good hearty breakfast. Perhaps this is why the Denver omelette is renowned. In most diners throughout the U.S., the Denver omelette is the largest omelette served—it's the one with the "works."

The Eggshell, run by the Waldman Family, was recommended to us by a friend who used to work with us. Whether you order an omelette, a fritatta (open faced Italian omelette), or pantry pancakes, you will be well fueled for a day in the mountains.

Park Lane Cafe and the *L.A. (Last American) Diner* are both owned by Bob Roehl. The former is in Denver, the latter in Boulder, about twenty miles north of Denver on State Highway 36. Boulder and the mountains to the west are worth the ride, and so is a trip to the L.A. Diner. All portions are large, prices are very reasonable, and homemade best describes the style at both places. The cheddar cheese muffins at Park Lane Cafe made our eyes roll, and our mouths water. To show there is more to eat here than breakfast, Bob contributed a recipe for "Shrimp Pièrre."

Dudley's is an example of elegant dining in a casual atmosphere. We're not sure if this is a reflection of the lifestyle of the city or of the owners of Dudley's, Blair Taylor and Thom Wise. Along with their chef, Fred Bramhall, they have created a restaurant featuring Nouvelle French cuisine in an atmosphere that is relaxing. The menu is in French, but there is no need to despair. If you don't read French, the waiters will be happy to recite the menu in English and explain how the dishes are prepared. It is a wonderful setting for a romantic evening.

People in Denver take "hanging around" seriously.

Photo by the author

HUITRES ÉLYSÉES
(Rich Cream Oyster Stew)

Dudley's Restaurant

1½ qt. heavy cream
1 cup oyster juice or clam juice
½ lb. sharp white cheddar cheese, grated
1 bunch scallions, green only, chopped
2 whole pimientos, diced
salt and white pepper
36 medium-sized oysters, shelled
½ lb. fresh spinach
2 T. Parmesan cheese, freshly grated
1 T. black lumpfish caviar

☐ Bring cream and oyster juice to a boil. Simmer 10 minutes. Preheat broiler. Add cheese, scallions and pimientos to cream and blend well. Season with salt and white pepper to taste. Place 6 oysters in each of six heated soup bowls. Pour 1 cup boiling sauce in each bowl. Place a few spinach leaves on top of each and top with 1 teaspoon Parmesan. Place under preheated broiler until lightly browned. Top each bowl with ½ teaspoon caviar and serve immediately. Serves 6.

SELLE D'AGNEAU DUXELLE EN FEUILLETÉ
(Saddle of Lamb in Puff Pastry)

Dudley's Restaurant

1 6–8 lb. double loin of lamb, boned (save for stock)
3 carrots, chopped
3 large onions
2 celery stalks, chopped
3 qt. water
1 bay leaf
1 tsp. whole peppercorns
6 sprigs parsley
3 cups red wine
½ tsp. dried rosemary or 1 tsp. fresh rosemary
½ tsp. dried thyme or 1 tsp. fresh thyme
salt and pepper
1 lb. fresh spinach, washed, dried, and finely chopped
½ lb. fresh mushrooms, diced
3 T. unsalted butter
2 sheets puff pastry, 10 in. x 15 in., ⅛ in. thick
1 large egg, beaten

☐ Chop 2 onions. Brown the lamb bones and trimmings, chopped onions, carrots, and celery in broiler until brown on all sides, about 15 minutes.

Combine in a stockpot with water, bay leaf, thyme, peppercorns and parsley. Simmer for 4–6 hours. Strain and refrigerate overnight.

Remove surface fat from stock. Bring stock to a boil over high heat and reduce to 3 cups.

Combine reduced stock, wine, rosemary, and thyme and bring to a boil. Reduce over high heat to 2 cups. Taste and correct seasonings with salt and pepper. Reserve.

Brown the outside of loins and flaps very quickly in a sauté pan over high heat to seal in juices.

Mince remaining onion. Sauté spinach, mushrooms, and minced onion in butter, until all moisture has evaporated.

Preheat oven to 400° F.

Place 1 loin, seared side down, on 1 sheet of puff pastry. Spread with a quarter of the spinach filling, top with a tenderloin, and spread with another quarter of the filling. Top this with the flap, seared side up. Wrap the meat in puff pastry, roll up and tuck in the edges, sealing with beaten egg. Brush entire puff pastry with beaten egg and place on greased baking sheet.

Repeat process with second loin, using remaining meat, filling and pastry.

Bake lamb in preheated oven for 40 minutes. Remove from oven and let rest 5 minutes. Slice each loin into 6 slices. Pour ¼ cup warm sauce on each of 6 warm plates. Top with 2 slices.

Note: This treatment is almost like a jellyroll.

ITALIAN FRITATTA

The Eggshell

3 eggs, blended with wire whip
3 oz. spicy Italian sausage, sliced
2 oz. mushrooms, sliced
3 oz. mozzarella cheese
4 oz. Italian sauce
½ tsp. basil
1 tsp. butter

☐　In 7½-inch frying pan, melt butter and pour in eggs, mushrooms and sausage. Cook till almost done (set all the way around the edges) and turn entire fritatta completely over in pan. Cook 1 minute more and turn back over. Top with sauce, mozzarella cheese and basil. Place under preheated broiler till cheese is melted and serve immediately.

(We make our own sauce, but there are plenty of good ones on the market).

DENVER OMELETTE

The Eggshell

3 eggs, blended with wire whip
1 oz. onion, diced
2 oz. green pepper, diced
2 oz. ham, diced
2 oz. sharp cheddar cheese, grated
1 tsp. butter

☐　Melt butter in 9-inch omelette pan. Pour in eggs and let cook until they begin to "set." With rubber spatula, lift edges and let uncooked egg run underneath. When almost done, spread onion, peppers, ham, and cheese over half of the omelette. Place omelette under preheated broiler, till cheese is melted. Fold, top with more cheese and pepper, place under broiler again till cheese is melted. Serve immediately. Serves 1.

SHRIMP PIÈRRE

The Park Lane Café

1 T. garlic powder, or 3–4 cloves garlic, minced
1 yellow onion, diced
½ cup fresh parsley, minced, or ¼ cup dried parsley flakes
1 tsp. dry mustard
1 tsp. salt
⅔ cup olive oil
1 tsp. concentrated lemon juice, or juice from 1 lemon
1 lb. large shrimp, peeled, cleaned and deveined
4 cups rice, cooked and hot

☐　Combine first eight ingredients in a very large bowl and mix thoroughly to make a marinade. Add shrimp and stir well. Allow to marinate in the refrigerator for at least 5 hours or overnight. Ten minutes before serving, pour shrimp and marinade into a large sauté or frying pan. Sauté over medium high heat for about 5 minutes or until shrimp are just done. Do not overcook. Serve over hot, cooked rice. Makes 4 servings. "Shrimp Pièrre" may be accompanied by fresh, steamed asparagus and garnished with purple grapes, if desired. It goes well with Orvietto or any other light, white wine.

CHEDDAR CHEESE MUFFINS

The Park Lane Café

4 cups flour
2½ T. baking powder
1½ tsp. salt
1½ tsp. MSG
5 eggs
1½ cups milk
½ cup butter, softened
4 cups cheddar cheese, finely grated

☐　Sift together first four ingredients. In separate bowl, mix together next four ingredients. Combine these two mixtures and mix thoroughly. Preheat oven to 350° F. Grease the *bottom only* of three muffin pans (one dozen muffins to each pan). Fill each tin three-quarters full and bake 25–30 minutes. Makes about 36 muffins. Cheddar cheese muffins should be served piping hot with butter and honey, if desired.

Note: This recipe is designed for high altitude baking. If being prepared at a low altitude, it may be necessary to adjust it by using somewhat less flour.

EGGS CAPE COD

The Last American Diner

4 English muffins, split
8 eggs, poached
12 oz. crabmeat, flaked and warmed
8 artichoke bottoms, fresh or frozen
2 cups hollandaise sauce
4–6 T. butter

☐　Have ready four small, shallow casserole dishes, or four large plates. Sauté muffins (cut side down) and artichoke bottoms in butter, on grill or in large sauté pan, over medium-high heat until muffins are golden brown and artichoke bottoms are hot. Place two muffin halves, cut side up, in each dish. Top each muffin half with one artichoke bottom, 1½ oz. crabmeat, and one poached egg. Spoon ½ cup hollandaise sauce over all. Makes 4 servings. "Eggs Cape Cod" are especially nice served with cottage fried potatoes or hash browns and a slice of melon. For brunch, the dish is complimented by champagne, a dry white wine, or a Ramos Fizz.

DETROIT

If a plane left downtown Detroit, heading south, which foreign country would it fly over first? Mexico? Cuba? The answer is Canada.

Settled originally by the French as a trading city because of its location on a waterway between two Great Lakes and two countries, it was held by the British in the Revolutionary War and the War of 1812.

On the ground where Fort Pontchartrain once stood is the present-day Hotel Pontchartrain. Some seventeen years ago when it was being constructed, the owners of the hotel approached the Muers, a food and beverage operation in the area. Joe and Bill Muer of *Joe Muer's Oyster House* passed up the hotel proposal, but Joe's son Chuck formed the C.A. Muer Corp., and went into business with the hotel. In 1969, he began to plan the first *Charley's Crab* restaurant. He asked Chef Larry Pagliara to create a soup that would be a "signature" item unique to his restaurants. Larry came up with a fish chowder, "Charley's Chowder," based on the Mediterranean fish soup he was raised on in Italy. It's a soup so hearty, people think it has a beef base.

All of the Muer restaurants have excellent food and service. We happen to like Charley's Crab in Troy, Michigan. It is close to the Pontiac Silverdome, home of the Detroit Lions and host to Super Bowl XVI.

Lake St. Clair, north of Detroit between Lake Huron and Lake Erie, isn't big enough to be one of the Great Lakes, but local boaters think it's pretty great. In a town suitably named St. Clair Shores is a spot called *Brownie's on the Lake*. In the summertime, people come by boat and moor at the dock behind Brownie's. It's a place to eat n' meet. The food is good and after dinner hours, the bar is very busy.

The Renaissance Center, downtown on the Detroit River, and Windsor, the quaint city across the river in Canada, have many fine restaurants. Finding one you like is a matter of a little detective work and a sense of adventure.

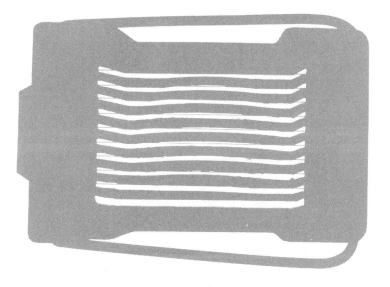

Detroit's Rennaissance Center has a number of fine restaurants.

ALMOND CHEESECAKE AMARETTO
Brownie's on the Lake

3 lb. Philadelphia cream cheese, room temperature
5 eggs
2½ cups sugar
4 oz. Amaretto
½ cup heavy cream

Crust
2 cups chocolate wafer crumbs
2 T. almond slivers
½ cup sugar
1 tsp. cinnamon
melted butter

Topping
1½ cups sour cream
½ cup sugar
2 oz. Amaretto
½ cup almond slivers, toasted

☐ Place cream cheese in a mixer. Blend at low speed till smooth. Add 2½ cups sugar and blend till sugar is dissolved, using a spatula to scrape down the sides and bottom of mixing bowl. Add 5 eggs, one at a time, blending well after each egg addition. Add 4 oz. Amaretto and whipping cream; blend at low speed for 7 minutes.

To make crust, mix all ingredients together and place in a 10 x 3 in. spring-form pan. Press firmly around the bottom and up the sides.

Refrigerate for 10 minutes, place cheese cake batter into pan, and bake at 375° F. for 1–1¼ hour. When cake is golden brown on top, shut off heat from oven and leave oven door open slightly. Let cake cool in oven (about 3 hours).

For the topping, mix all ingredients and spread over cake. Spread almonds around top edge of cake. Cover with wax paper and refrigerate overnight before cutting. Serves 16–18.

CHARLEY'S CHOWDER

Charlie's Crab

2 oz. olive oil, (by volume)
3 cloves garlic, crushed
2 oz. onions, (by weight), finely chopped
3 oz. celery, (by weight), finely chopped
pinch each: oregano, basil, and thyme
6 oz. stewed tomatoes, (by volume) very finely
    chopped
3 pt. water
3 pt. clam juice (if not available, use Clamato juice)
1 lb. boneless fish (pollack or turbot)
1 oz. parsley, (by weight), finely chopped
Salt to taste

☐ Place olive oil in large pot, heat on stove until very hot. Drop into the hot oil the crushed garlic cloves, and cook the garlic until golden in color. It is important that you do not burn the garlic as this will ruin the taste. Remove the cloves from the oil. While the oil is hot, add the onions and cook for a minute or two. Add the basil, oregano, and thyme and cook for another minute. Add the celery and cook until translucent in color. Add the finely chopped tomatoes and cook for about 20–25 minutes, stirring to prevent sticking.

Add water, fish, clam juice and cook for an additional 15 minutes, uncovered at full heat. This process will remove moisture, purify and extract oils for flavoring the chowder. Add salt, cover the pot and keep cooking for another 20 minutes at low heat. Stir often by whipping to break up the fish and blend the flavor. When serving, add the chopped parsley.

Note: When serving this soup as an appetizer, use parsley as the recipe indicates. If using as the court bouillon for bouillabaisse, eliminate the chopped parsley.

DEVILED CRAB BALLS

Joe Muer's Restaurant

1½ lb. three-day-old bread
5 eggs, hard cooked and chopped
1 heaping T. salt
1 heaping T. dry mustard
1 large onion, chopped and sautéed in butter
1¼ oz. Worcestershire sauce
1¼ oz. vinegar
3 T. mayonnaise
2 lb. fresh crab meat, shredded

☐ Cut crusts from bread and crumble into small bits in large mixing bowl. Add eggs, salt, mustard and mix well. Mix in onions, Worcestershire sauce, vinegar and mayonnaise. Add crab meat by gently folding into other ingredients. Form the mixture as you would small snowballs. Place on baking sheets; bake at 350°F. for 15–20 minutes. Makes about 40 balls. Serve hot with mustard sauce.

Pontiac Silverdome provides a welcome change of climate for the Lions and Vikings, two venerable foul-weather foes.

GREEN BAY

Recorded history of the area began when a French explorer named Jean Nicolet stepped ashore, just northeast of the present city in 1634. He had been sent by the governor of Quebec to search for a sea route to the Orient, and claim the land for France. He called the area *La Baye Verte,* for the greenish waters of the bay in spring and summer.

In the mid-1800s, German, Irish, Belgian, and Polish immigrants poured in to work at farming and logging. The first paper mills were built around the turn of the century. Food products are produced and packaged here. Cheese is produced in five plants, meat in four, dairy products (other than cheese) in six, canning in two and pickles in three. It's no wonder their football team began as a semi-pro team from a local packing plant.

Jean Nicolet may have named the town, but it was Vince Lombardi and the Green Bay Packers who "put the town on the map." Green Bay is the smallest of the pro-football cities; nonetheless, the "Pack" has brought home eleven world championships. Milwaukee hosts some of the home games, and for this reason we have included restaurants from that city as well.

Two famous restaurants representing the German influence in Milwaukee are *John Ernst Café* and *Mader's Restaurant.* In 1878, *Mother Heiser's Place* was opened and operated under that name until 1938, when John and Ida Ernst took over. Since then, it has been handed down to their daughter, Marianne, and her husband, Erwin Lindenberg, and finally to their sons, Jim and John. The Old World German atmosphere remains, along with their concept of quality and service. They sent an entire meal of recipes to include in our book.

Mader's has a family history as well. Started as *The Comfort* by Charles Mader in 1902, the restaurant has grown along with the family and now Charles's grandson, Victor, manages the place. Victor's father, Gustave, travels back and forth from Europe, searching out new recipes and wines, four of which are bottled under Mader's label. Along with many awards for restaurant excellence, the walls of the restaurant are covered with artwork from Europe, as well as medieval German weaponry. The meal of recipes representing Mader's is from a cookbook of their own, sold at the restaurant.

A book on Monday Night Football would not be complete without mentioning Bob Uecker. Whenever one of our cameras focuses on someone or something really bizarre in the stands, you'll most likely hear one of the announcers quip "Well, Uecker's here tonight." In Bob's honor, we're including a restaurant he told us about. Bob's friend, Rick Falzarano, runs an Italian place, *Del Mondo Ristorante,* that some claim is the best in the Midwest. We know that Bob has spent enough time in Milwaukee to know where to get the best. We agree that the food is great.

One of two favorite places in Green Bay is the *John Nero Restaurant* on Military Avenue. Their addition to the book is an interesting one, "Cream of Reuben Soup." It is a meal in itself. We've seen soup 'n' sandwich specials, but this is the first time we've seen the sandwich in the soup!

Our other Green Bay favorite is the *Hansen House.* Chef John Von Sickle showed us how they do prime rib, and "Veal Oscar."

Here are some hearty meals from an area where many calories a day are burned just battling the cold. The locals like it—there's never a worry about the beer getting warm!

GREEN BAY

Dinner for Six at John Ernst Café

Beef Consommé with Liver Dumplings
Spinach Salad with Hot Bacon Dressing
Jaeger Schnitzel
Spaetzels
Mocha Torte
Suggested Wines
Preceding the entree: Oestreicher Lenchen Riesling 1979. With entree: Johannisberger Erntebringer Riesling Kabinett 1978.

BEEF CONSOMMÉ

John Ernst Café

4–5 lb. fresh cracked beef bones
2 large onions, quartered
2 carrots, coarsely chopped
2 parsley roots, coarsely chopped, with about ⅓ cup stems and leaves from tops
3 celery stalks, coarsely chopped
2 tomatoes, coarsely chopped
2 T. beef bouillon granules
1 tsp. whole peppercorns
4 qt. cold water

☐ In a roasting pan, brown the beef bones at 450° F for about ½ hour until nut brown. Add ½ cup of water to the roasting pan while still hot to deglaze.

Add the bones and liquid to the stock pot along with all the above. Bring to a boil, then simmer for about 5 hours.

Strain the consommé through a sieve lined with a damp white cotton cloth or a coffee filter. Yields 3 quarts.

LIVER DUMPLINGS FOR SOUP

John Ernst Café

1½ cups raw livers, washed (we use chicken and turkey)
1 onion, sliced
4 T. butter
1 hard roll, softened in water, and squeezed dry
1 cup bread or roll crumbs
5 large sprigs of parsley
½ cup all-purpose flour

1 egg
1 tsp. salt
¼ tsp. ground pepper
1 pinch sweet marjoram
½ pinch sweet basil

☐ Sauté onions in butter until tan (not brown). Put aside in a large mixing bowl. Grind raw livers, parsley, sautéed onions and softened roll, twice. Add salt, pepper, and herbs. Mix well. Add egg and mix again. Now add the flour and enough bread crumbs to make mixture the consistency of a sticky bread dough—not too moist, nor too dry. Let mixture rest for ½ hour.

Using a teaspoon, scoop some of the batter and roll it along the edge of the bowl, achieving the shape of a small football. Drop from the spoon into the salted boiling water. Try one first. You may want to add more bread crumbs to tighten the batter. Smaller size is better than larger because they swell. Cook gently for about 15–20 minutes. Cool under cold water if you make them ahead of time.

Serve in beef consommé. Yields approximately 18–20 dumplings. *Note:* Dumplings may be made larger and served with sauerkraut. Cooking time will be longer.

SPINACH SALAD WITH HOT BACON DRESSING

John Ernst Café

2–2½ lb. fresh leaf spinach with stems removed, cleaned and dried, leaves left whole
2 ripened tomatoes, cut into 12 wedges
2 hard-boiled eggs cut into 12 slices (coins)
12 slices lean bacon, fried crispy and towel drained and crumbled (reserve one-half the rendered bacon fat and allow to cool slightly)
1 cup cold water
¾ cup white vinegar
¾ cup sugar
¾ tsp. salt
1 T. corn starch

☐ In a *stainless steel* saucepan, combine the corn starch, cold water, sugar and salt. Heat to boiling. Slowly add the reserved bacon fat (never add the fat if it's hot; it will splatter and may flare). Add the vinegar. Bring to a boil and remove from the heat. Allow to cool, but keep warm.

Arrange the spinach leaves on a salad plate. Add the hot dressing over the leaves.

Sprinkle with crumbled bacon pieces. Garnish with tomatoes and egg slices. Serves 4.

JAEGER SCHNITZEL

John Ernst Café

3 lb. premium veal tenderloin or cross grain slices from the inside of the round.

3 oz. butter, clarified (by volume)
1 cup flour
paprika
salt

Sauce

2 oz. butter, clarified (by volume)
½–¾ cup shallots, finely minced
⅓ cup all-purpose flour
1½ T. tomato purée
3½ cups veal demi-glace (see note below)
1 lb. fresh mushrooms, cleaned and halved (lengthwise)
1 cup Chablis
½ tsp. salt

☐ In a 4-quart sauce pan, over low heat, sauté the shallots in the clarified butter till transparent. Add the flour and whisk. Allow the roux to cook 4–5 minutes but do not allow to brown. Add the tomato purée and whisk.

Add one-half the demi-glace and whisk. Add the remaining glace and blend. Allow the sauce to come to a low boil, then simmer, whisking from time to time to prevent sticking. Add the mushrooms and Chablis. Salt to taste. (Do not allow the sauce to simmer long. Serve shortly within 1 hour of preparing.)

Cut veal into 4 oz. slices and pound with flat side of a cleaver or mallet. Sprinkle each cutlet with salt and paprika and dredge in flour. Sauté the cutlets in clarified butter till cooked through and are golden brown. Hold sautéed cutlet in a 200° F oven until all are sautéed.

Arrange two cutlets and spaetzels (see recipe following) on a plate and ladle about 4 ounces of mushroom rich sauce over the veal. Garnish with parsley and serve.

Note: Recipe for veal demi-glace is same as for Beef Consommé, except substitute veal bones for beef. Then *simmer* finished stock an additional 1–1½ hours to reduce its volume and strengthen flavors.

SPAETZELS

John Ernst Café

3 cups all-purpose flour
4 eggs
4 oz. cold water
2 T. salt

☐ Fill a 6-quart pot two-thirds full with hot water and add the salt. Bring to a rolling boil while preparing the batter.

Combine the eggs and water with a whisk until thoroughly mixed. Add the flour, one cup at a time, and blend each cup thoroughly using a stiff wooden spoon.

If you have a spaetzel mill, mill the batter into the rapidly boiling, salted water. If not, place the batter in a good quality plastic bag. Snip one corner for a hole

about the diameter of a pencil and squeeze the batter into the boiling water.

Let the water return to a boil. Simmer for 1 minute. Pour the spaetzels into a sieve and shower with cold water till they are cold to the touch. Refrigerate.

To reheat the spaetzels, place them in a sieve and either shower with hot water or set the sieve in a pan of hot water.

Serve hot spaetzels plain or toss in butter. Makes 4 to 6 servings.

MOCHA TORTE

John Ernst Café

6 eggs at room temperature, separated
1 T. plus 1 tsp. cold water
1½ tsp. vanilla
1 cup cake flour, unsifted or 1 cup plus 2 T. sifted flour
1 cup super fine sugar
½ tsp. salt
1 T. baking powder

☐ Preheat oven to 375° F. Grease and flour two 9-inch cake pans. Combine yolks, cold water, salt and vanilla. Whisk smooth. Set aside.

Sift cake flour and baking powder together. Set aside. Place sugar in a convenient container to aid pouring and reserve.

Beat egg whites till soft peaks form. Slowly add sugar and mix well. Slowly add the yolk mixture. Mix at slow speed till yolks are thoroughly blended with the whites. At the mixer's slowest speed, add the flour. Do not over-mix at this point. Only blend the flour, then stop. Batter should be light and airy.

Divide the batter between the two pans. Bake 30 minutes. Tops should be almond brown.

Invert cakes onto wax paper. Cool on racks. When cool, slice each cake into three layers.

Frosting

1 lb. sweet cream butter, unsalted, at room temperature (70°–75° F)
½ lb. powdered sugar
1 egg yolk
3 oz. plus 1 T. very strong black coffee (cold)

☐ In a mixing bowl, cream the butter and egg yolk till nearly white in color. Slowly add the powdered sugar and coffee alternately, until all ingredients are blended. Try to finish with sugar as the last ingredient.

To assemble, remove the wax paper without peeling the top layers off the cakes. Reserve the best layer of cake (nicely browned) for the top. Frost each layer, then assemble the next. You may frost the exterior of the torte if you like, but it's not necessary. We don't. If you decide to frost it, use the butter cream to frost and decorate with coffee-chocolate icing. Highlight each slice with one or two candy coffee beans.

HOUSTON

The largest city in Texas is named after the general of the Texas army, Sam Houston, who won independence from Mexico. What is now headquarters for the NASA's Johnson Space Center was a riverboat landing in 1836. The city is the financial, shipping, and industrial center of the state. It's hard to think of Houston without thinking about oil. The derricks are here, the money is here, and the Houston Oilers are here. And its restaurants represent some of these influences.

The riverboat feeling still is alive just down the road from the Houston Astrodome. We know that in Texas, "just down the road" can be twenty miles, but this place is very close. It's called *Captain Benny's,* and it represents freshness. This is a standup seafood bar in an old boat—if you're tall, you'd better not stand up too straight. But if you are 6'5" or taller, you can probably lean on the bar anywhere you want! There you'll find fresh chowder, gumbo, oysters on the half shell, shrimp, and ice cold beer. This is not a place for a quiet dinner for two; it's a place for fresh seafood and fun.

A place for a quiet dinner is *Nick's Fishmarket.* Serving a sixty-item menu as does its sister restaurant in Chicago, Nick's also has the private booths, phone jacks, and dimmer switches for menu reading and romantic dining. There also are private dinner rooms available including the "Oval Office," an extravagantly decorated room seating from two to eight. Featuring Clarence House mohair wall coverings, hand-woven Edward Fields carpeting, a Willy Riggs granite table, Karl Springer goatskin Onassis chairs, custom made Porthault linens, Tiffany silver and Baccarat crystal, the room is furnished at approximately $30,000 a seat. The only thing that could make the room more elegant in our minds is to be able to afford dining there. Perhaps if everyone bought another of these guides for a friend. . . .

Pete Dominguez has *Casa Dominguez* in Houston in addition to his Dallas restaurants. This chapter features "Mexican Pete-Za," a dish named after Pete.

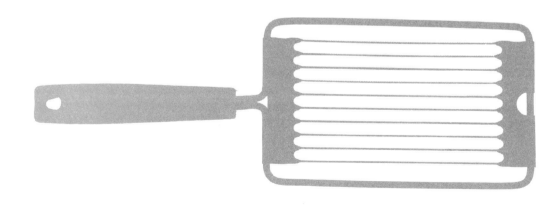

Seats are hard to come by at Captain Benny's standup seafood bar, but freshness is guaranteed.

Photo by the author

FISHMARKET CATFISH

Nick's Fishmarket

2 lb. catfish filets
seasoned flour
2 eggs, beaten
¾ cup vegetable oil

☐ Dust fish filets with seasoned flour. Dip in eggs, then in flour. Heat vegetable oil until very hot. Add fish and sauté until golden on both sides (7–10 minutes). Remove to heated platter. Spoon dill sauce over fish filets and garnish with lemon wedges and parsley. Makes 4–6 servings.

Dill Sauce

¼ cup butter
1 T. lemon juice
½ tsp. chopped dill
¼ cup brown sauce (recipe below)

Heat butter and lemon juice. Add dill, stir in demi-glace. Cook and stir until heated through and blended.

Brown Sauce (Demi-Glace)

¼ cup butter or margarine
6 T. flour
2 cubes beef bouillon
2½ cups boiling water
2 parsley sprigs
1 tsp. soy sauce

Dissolve bouillon cubes in boiling water and add parsley. Simmer 10 minutes. Remove parsley and return to boil. In a separate pan, melt butter and stir in flour to make a thick paste. Add this mixture to boiling bouillon, add soy sauce, and stir until glace has reached a medium consistency. Refrigerate extra demi-glace and serve, after reheating, as a garnish with other seafoods.

BUNUEIOS

Casa Dominguez

flour tortillas
cooking oil
sugar-cinnamon mixture
honey, to taste

☐ Use about a 12-inch skillet. Pour cooking oil about 1 inch deep, heat to 360° F. Cut tortillas into fourths, carefully place two pieces at a time into oil and scoop oil over top. Turn bunueios with tongs and fry other side until crisp. Drain on paper towels. Sprinkle hot bunueios immediately with sugar-cinnamon mixture. Pour honey to taste and serve.

PICO DE GALLO
(Rooster's Beak)

½ onion, chopped
2 tomatoes, diced
½ cup loosely packed cilantro leaves, coarsely chopped
2 hot green peppers or smaller amount, to taste

☐ Mix tomatoes, onion, cilantro and hot peppers. Squeeze lemon juice over vegetables. Add salt to taste, stir. Serve immediately or refrigerate. Makes about 2 cups. This fresh vegetable salsa enhances any Mexican dish. Dip into with tortilla chips, or add to food for spice.

POACHED MAHI MAHI VERONIQUE
Nick's Fishmarket

Fish Stock

1 gal. water
2 carrots
1 onion, quartered
4 celery stalks
1½ lb. fish bones or fish heads
1 cup white wine

☐ Put all ingredients in a stock pot. Let simmer for 30 minutes. Drain vegetables and fish from stock and keep the liquid.

Fish

12 4-oz. pieces mahi mahi
½ cup white wine
1 bay leaf

In a pan large enough to hold 12 pieces of fish, cover fish with water. Add wine and bay leaf. Put in oven for 20 minutes at 450° F.

Cream Sauce

1 cup vegetable oil
¾ cup flour
½ gal. milk
1 qt. fish stock
salt and pepper, to taste

☐ To prepare a roux, heat vegetable oil in a pot, remove from flame and slowly add flour while stirring constantly to a pasty consistency. Set aside. Heat milk in a separate pot. Add fish stock and seasoning to milk, thicken with roux. (Extra roux, if any, can be stored in the refrigerator for later use.)

Remove fish from pan and put two pieces on each plate. Cover with cream sauce and add seedless white grapes (about 12 per serving). Dish serves 6.

MEXICAN PETE-ZA
Casa Dominguez

6 flour tortillas
¼ lb. provolone cheese
1 lb. hamburger meat
2 tomatoes, diced
½ small onion
jalapenos, if desired

☐ Cook hamburger meat in an open skillet. Add salt and pepper to taste, onion and tomatoes. Add ½ cup water, and stir. Cook for 10 minutes.

Use a 12-inch sheet of foil, spread lightly with butter. Place 1 flour tortilla on it. Cover with hamburger meat, add provolone cheese to cover hamburger meat, add small amount of diced tomatoes and onion to taste and add jalapenos, if desired hot. Spread another tortilla with butter and place on top. Place in oven until tortilla is crisp. Cut in quarters. Garnish with guacamole on a bed of lettuce.

Photo by ABC Sports

Earl Campbell anchors Houston's offense. No wonder fans call the team the Houston "Earlers."

53

KANSAS CITY

Named after the Kansas Indians, Kansas City began as a fur-trading post in the 1820s. The nation's first suburban shopping center was begun here in the 1920s. Country Club Plaza was conceived by J.C. Nichols Sr. The Spanish theme with its red tiled roofs, mosaics, and colorful buildings provides an architectural continuity that distinguishes "The Plaza." The area is filled with fountains and statues which add to the ambience.

The Harry S. Truman Sports Complex, outside Kansas City, is an amazing architectural feat. Dual stadiums house the baseball Royals in Royal Stadium, and the football Chiefs in Arrowhead Stadium. Across the street from the complex, the Sheraton Royale houses a restaurant called the *Remington*. The food featured here takes the imagination back to the days of Dodge City, home of the likes of Wyatt Earp, Doc Holiday, and Bat Masterson. You can order rattlesnake meat for an appetizer, or buffalo steak for the main course—good buffalo steak. Somehow, mako shark is also available. It's definitely not a local fish, but it sure is good.

A local specialty, probably begun in the days when Kansas City had the second largest livestock exchange in the United States, is barbecue sauce. If you love barbecued food, you'd better not leave without some Gates' Barbecue Sauce. You can buy it by the bottle at a *Gates and Sons*. We couldn't get Mrs. Gates to give us the secret recipe, so we asked our friend Wesley Kabler for his. Wes, a friend of ours from Lawrence, Kansas, has been meeting us in Indianapolis for years during race week at the 500. We're out there for our Wide World of Sports race coverage and Wes is there, cooking up barbecue, Nevada Annie's Chili, and spreading good cheer. His barbecue sauce is no secret, unlike most in Kansas, and we're thankful he's been so generous with it over the years.

Stop in the *Purple Pig* or the *Flamingo Club* in Lawrence sometime and say hello. Neither is a place for dinner. You'll more than likely find mud wrestling or some other form of madness going on. Doc Holiday and Bat Masterson may be long gone, but you can be sure there are still a few wild men roaming the Western Plains.

Meierhoff's is a German restaurant we like for both food and service. Bob Phomiel sent us a recipe for potato pancakes, a specialty at the restaurant.

Last but not least is Andy's Italian selection, *Jasper's*. They prepare their veal with eggplant and lemon and call it "Vitello Limonata con Melangone Dore."

Kansas City is one place with no scheduling problems when baseball stretches into the football season.

WESLEY'S BARBECUE SAUCE

Wesley Kabler

2 tsp. sugar
1 tsp. salt
⅛ tsp. red pepper
1 tsp. black pepper
1 T. dry mustard
1 tsp. chili powder
2 T. vinegar
½ tsp. Tabasco sauce
1 T. Worcestershire sauce
1 cup water
1 T. onion, chopped
1 clove garlic, minced

☐ Mix everything together and work 4–5 minutes. Then spread it on anything to barbecue.

NEVADA ANNIE'S CHILI

Wesley Kabler

1 large onion, coarsely chopped (1 cup)
1 green pepper, chopped (1 cup)
1 large celery stalk, chopped
1 large clove garlic, minced
3 T. vegetable oil
4 lb. ground beef/chuck

1½ tsp. jalapeno pepper, minced (fresh or canned)
½ cup chili powder
1 T. ground cumin
1 tsp. garlic salt
1 tsp. onion salt
1 tsp. liquid red pepper seasoning
1½ bay leaves, crumbled
2 tsp. salt (or more, to taste)
¼ tsp. freshly ground black pepper
⅔ cup beer
1 16-oz. can stewed tomatoes
1 8-oz. can tomato sauce
1 6-oz. can tomato paste
2 T. honey
1½ cups water

☐ Stir fry the onion, green pepper, celery, and garlic in the oil in a large kettle or Dutch oven 8 minutes or until tender and golden. Add beef and cook, breaking up large clumps until no pink remains. Add jalapeno, chili powder, cumin, garlic and onion salts, red pepper seasonings, bay leaves, salt, pepper, beer, tomatoes, tomato sauce and paste, honey, and enough water to come just to the top of the chili ingredients. Simmer uncovered very slowly, stirring often, for at least 3 hours or until chili is thick and flavors are well blended. Add more salt if needed. Serves 8–10.

VITELLO LIMONATA CON MELANZANA DORE

Jasper's

8 slices veal scallopine (approximately 1¼ pounds)
salt and freshly ground pepper, to taste
½ pound eggplant, peeled and cut into eight ¼" rounds
flour for dredging
2 eggs, slightly beaten
1 cup fine fresh breadcrumbs
½ cup plus 3 T. peanut oil or corn oil
1 T. butter
8 thin slices of lemon
1 tsp. oregano
1 T. finely chopped parsley

Pound the veal lightly with a flat mallet, then sprinkle with salt and pepper. Sprinkle sliced eggplant with salt and pepper, then dredge in flour and shake off excess. Dip eggplant in egg, then in breadcrumbs. Pat to help the crumbs adhere. Then heat ½ cup of oil and cook the eggplant pieces on both sides until golden brown. Drain on paper towels.

Dip the veal in flour and shake off excess. Dip in egg and coat each piece completely. Heat the 3 T. of oil and the butter in a skillet and cook the veal, two slices at a time, until golden on both sides.

Arrange the veal on a platter, slightly overlapping the slices. Top each slice with an eggplant round and a lemon slice. Sprinkle with oregano and parsley and serve hot.

POTATO PANCAKES

Meierhoff's

5 medium potatoes
3 medium onions
6 eggs
1 cup vegetable oil
1 cup flour
½ T. salt
½ tsp. white pepper
2 T. Accent
1 tsp. onion powder
1 tsp. garlic powder

Grate potatoes, with skin on, along with onions, on a fine grater. Place onions and potatoes in mixing bowl.

Beat the eggs and add, along with vegetable oil, to the potato and onion mixture. Blend well, then mix in flour. Add remaining ingredients and stir well. Fry on hot griddle or pan, browning both sides, and serve with sour cream or applesauce.

Country Club Plaza, as we've already noted, was the highlight of our KC trip.

LOS ANGELES

Hollywood, Disneyland, warm weather, palm trees, and freeways. Out-of-towners discover quickly that Los Angeles is more complex than the images it evokes; in fact, it is a mind-boggling place for a non-Angelino. Where else can you go skiing in the morning and surfing in the afternoon? The Los Angeles area is so large that the football franchise moved south a good forty-minute drive on the freeway, and the team is still called the Los Angeles Rams.

The Spanish founded the city in the 1780s, but it wasn't until the 1880s that it began to boom. Many took advantage of a rate war on the railroads; a person could travel from Kansas City to Los Angeles for one dollar, and thousands did. Even today's airfare battles can't beat that.

Many immigrants from Asia came to the United States and settled in this West Coast city. Two more booms in the 1920s and 1950s brought Los Angeles to the third most populated city in the U.S. (It just recently beat out Chicago for the number two spot.) Some came for the climate, some to work in the factories, and some to find fame on the silver screen.

In Beverly Hills at the head of La Cienaga Boulevard's "Restaurant Row" stands *Lawry's The Prime Rib*. As mentioned in the Chicago chapter, Laurence L. Frank was an innovator who deserves credit as one of the most famous restaurateurs in America. We offer two prime rib side dishes from Lawry's.

Don Meredith knows his way around town, and recommends *La Scala,* also in Beverly Hills. He asked them to send recipes for his favorites

and they obliged. *Man Fook Low* is a Chinese restaurant the crew found in the days when the Rams were still in the Coliseum. Frank Kum tells you how to prepare "Almond Chicken" and "Asparagus Beef." He also reminded us of his other restaurants in the area serving the same delicious food. *The Pear Blossom* is in Westwood, along with a *Wok Inn.* There are two more Wok Inns in Los Angeles and Santa Barbara.

One month before Disneyland opened its doors in 1955, the Belisle family opened their restaurant just down the street. Harvey and Charlotte Belisle wrote on the back of their menus, "Serving excellent food made with the very finest ingredients is still our main concern." And Harvey insists on it. The portions at *Belisle's* are more than generous. Harvey grew up on a farm in Wisconsin (See Green Bay, "hearty eaters"). He used to help his mother prepare meals for the hungry farm hands, and those fellows could eat!

They bake all their own "Mile High Pies" and "Giant Cookies," the names of which are no exaggeration. Jim Heneghan (our Pizzaria #Uno's taster) discovered Belisle's years ago when working on the crew that built Disneyland, and this fellow can eat, too!

When we were there, we eyed the "Mile High Pies" but after something like the "Farmer's Omelette," it was all we could do just to get up, and we fellas can eat! Belisle's is not a hard place to find—after 25 years it's still painted pink. Well, as anyone from east of the San Andreas fault would say, "Hey, it's California."

The Rams left the Los Angeles Coliseum for Anaheim, but they took their name with them.

MELENZANA NOSTRA

La Scala

¼ cup olive oil
1 eggplant, peeled and cut in ½"·cubes
½ small onion, finely chopped
1 ripe tomato, peeled and chopped
½ tsp. oregano
salt and pepper, to taste
½ cup imported Parmesan cheese
1½ cups béchamel sauce
½ cup sauce Espanol (spicy tomato sauce)
12 very thin crepes (6 inch)
12 slices fontina cheese, 1½ x 1½ in.

☐ In a large skillet, heat oil and sauté onion; when slightly browned, add eggplant and sauté until tender. Add tomato and spices and stir a little. Add 3 tablespoons of cheese and ½ cup bechamel sauce and toss well. Place last mixture in blender and blend until smooth. Place crepes on the table, put a spoonful of mixture on each crepe and fold them into squares. Arrange the filled crepes on a baking dish and place a slice of fontina cheese on top of each crepe. Cover with the balance of the béchamel sauce & sauce Espanol. Sprinkle with remaining Parmesan cheese and bake for about 10 minutes.

FARMER'S OMELETTE

Belisle's

3 eggs
3 heaping T. tomatoes, diced
3 heaping T. onions, diced
3 heaping T. fresh mushrooms, sliced and sautéed
½ cup hash browns, freshly browned
½ cup cheddar cheese, grated
1 T. vegetable oil
1 T. water

☐ Break eggs, and whip briskly in large bowl. Add tomatoes, onions, mushrooms, and hash browns and stir together.

Put large frying pan over medium fire. When hot, add oil and distribute it evenly over the entire surface. Pour contents of bowl into pan, and distribute evenly over the entire surface. When eggs have set about halfway or three-quarters up from bottom, and are still a little runny on top, insert two spatulas under omelette and flip over.

Immediately put cheese over top of omelette, add water, cover pan and remove from heat. After thirty seconds, remove from pan, open faced on large dinner plate. Garnish with orange slice and sprig of fresh parsley or mint, and serve.

ENGLISH TRIFLE

Lawry's The Prime Rib

1 4½-oz. package vanilla pudding and pie filling mix
2 cups light cream
2 T. dark Puerto Rican Rum
2¼ cups heavy cream
3 T. sugar
2 T. red raspberry preserves
1 10-inch round sponge cake
¼ cup brandy
¼ cup dry sherry
30 whole strawberries

☐ Combine pudding mix and light cream. Cook, stirring constantly, until mixture comes to a boil and thickens. Add rum; chill. Whip 1¼ cups heavy cream and 1 tablespoon sugar until stiff. Fold into chilled pudding. Coat the inside of a deep 10-inch bowl with raspberry preserves to within 1-inch of the top. Slice cake horizontally into fourths. Place top slice, crust side up, in bottom of bowl, curving edges of cake upward.

Combine brandy and sherry, sprinkle about a fourth of the mixture (about 1 tablespoon) over the cake slice. Spread one third of chilled pudding mixture over cake slice. Repeat procedure two additional times. Arrange 15 strawberries on top layer of pudding. Cover with remaining cake layer, crust side down. Sprinkle with remaining brandy-sherry mixture.

Whip remaining 1 cup cream and 2 tablespoons sugar until stiff. Place whipped cream in pastry bag with fluted tip. Make 12 mounds around edge of bowl and 3 mounds across diameter. Top each mound with a strawberry. Chill at least 6 hours. To serve: spoon onto chilled dessert plates. Serves 12.

ALMOND CHICKEN

Man Fook Low

8 oz. white chicken meat, diced
2 oz. bamboo shoots, diced
2 oz. water chestnuts, diced
2 oz. celery, diced
1 egg white
1 tsp. sherry
1 pinch salt
1 pinch white pepper
¼ tsp. MSG
4 T. peanut oil
2 oz. roasted almonds
2 tsp. soy sauce
1 tsp. cornstarch

☐ Mix cornstarch, soy sauce and 2 tablespoons water, set aside. Add egg white, sherry, salt, pepper to chicken, mix well. Heat peanut oil in frying pan and stir fry chicken until done, remove.

Put diced celery, bamboo shoots and water chestnuts in frying pan. Add ¼ cup water, cover and cook for 2 minutes. Add ¼ teaspoon monosodium glutamate and chicken, stir. Add mixture of cornstarch, soy sauce and water, stir till mixture thickens. Place on platter and sprinkle almonds on top. Serves 2.

CHICKEN LA SCALA

La Scala

2 2½-lb. chickens, boned, skinned, and cubed
2 chicken livers, finely chopped
½ tsp. oregano
2 large shallots, finely chopped
4 oz. sherry
½ cup chicken broth
1 large potato, cut into balls, then fried
salt and pepper, to taste

☐ In a heavy skillet, warm some oil and sauté chicken until brown. Drain oil, add shallots, chicken livers, oregano, salt and pepper. Mix well and add sherry. Flambé, then add chicken broth, potato and cook for five minutes, or until sauce reduces to one third. Serves 4.

ASPARAGUS BEEF

Man Fook Low

8 oz. frozen asparagus, cut in 1½-in. pieces
8 oz. sirloin or flank steak, cut to ½ x ½ x ¾ in.
1 tsp. fermented black bean (spice, or bean sauce)
1 clove garlic, minced
½ tsp. salt
¼ tsp. monosodium glutamate
2 tsp. soy sauce
4 T. peanut oil
1 tsp. cornstarch
¼ cup water

☐ Mix cornstarch, soy sauce and 2 tablespoons water; set aside. Put peanut oil in hot frying pan, add garlic, fermented black bean, and salt. Add beef, stir, add asparagus, stir, add water. Cover and cook for 2 minutes. Add monosodium glutamate and cornstarch mixture and stir till mixture thickens.

YORKSHIRE PUDDING

Lawry's The Prime Rib

1 cup minus 1 tsp. sifted Flour
½ tsp. salt
2 eggs, beaten
¾ cup milk   ¾ cup water

☐ Sift flour and salt together; make a well, add eggs. Blend together and add milk and water slowly, beating continuously. If using an electric mixer, beat at high speed for at least 10 minutes (very important to beat a long time). Let stand for an hour. Heat oven to 450° F. Place a 5-inch omelette pan in oven to heat. When hot, coat the pan with oil, heat again. Pour ½ cup batter into pan; bake for 35 minutes. Serves 4.

MIAMI

It is our theory that the television character "Flipper" had a lot to do with Miami's football team being named the Dolphins. One of Flipper's friends from the Seaquarium on Key Biscayne used to watch the football games from a tank in the endzone at the Orange Bowl. If Garo Yepremian kicked an extra point into the tank, the dolphin would·flip the ball out to a trainer with either its nose or tail. After a flip or two of its own, it usually received a standing ovation from the crowd.

The Florida Keys, the group of islands just south of Miami, were full of adventure long before Flipper or television. A fleet of Spanish treasure galleons was sunk in a hurricane there in 1733. Some of the treasure was recovered 222 years later. Gold doubloons, pieces of eight, silver bars weighing 60 to 75 pounds, along with jewelry, cannons, swords, and an anchor are on display at McKee's Museum of Sunken Treasure on Plantation Key.

For dining, there is another treasure on Plantation Key, *Marker 88.* Chef and owner André Mueller offers gourmet dining in a relaxed, casual atmosphere. The interior is serenely tropical, and André says come early to watch the sun set on the Gulf of Mexico. He passed along some local favorites: "Conch Bisque," "Yellowtail Rangoon," and "Mangoes Morada" (sort of a "Mangoes Foster," oh yumm!). The "Key Lime Pie" is not too shabby either. All the recipes can be adjusted to available items in case conch, yellowtail, or mangoes aren't available where you are. (That André thinks of everything.) The drive to the Keys is worth it.

In North Miami, on Arthur Godfrey Boulevard, is another treasure. There is a wine cellar, the contents of which are worth over a million dollars. The stock includes a collection of Chateau Lafite Rothschild, beginning with a Red Bordeaux 1822 vintage priced at $31,000. This is at *The Forge,* a favorite spot of ABC Sports for years. The bistro-type hand-chiseled bar (a band actually plays behind the bar) is a topnotch watering hole.

Originally it was the site of a forge where Dino Phillips created ornaments, gates, and torches for the estates of the Gatsby era. In the 1930s there was a gambling casino above the opulence of the restaurant. There are Tiffany lamps, crystal goblets, hand-loomed tablecloths, brass rails from old ships, each decked with European art nouveau bronzes. The velvet booths and Viennese antique chandeliers add to the effect.

But you may ask, how's the food at The Forge? They call the cuisine "sophisticated American, liberally dotted with unusual Continental Nouvelle Cuisine specialties." Try the "Artichoke Hearts Monte Carlo" recipe for an appetizer. Crepes are also featured for appetizers and dessert. Our favorite dessert from The Forge is their "Blacksmith's Pie." Pure heaven. Or, how about a pear poached in champagne? David Kurtz, manager, Philip Wocker, maitre d', and Toni Hipp, executive chef, must be congratulated for The Forge's four-star rating by the *Mobil Travel Guide,* to say nothing of *our* recommendation.

It is impossible these days to visit Miami without feeling the Latin influence. To get a taste of Spanish Basque or Cuban cooking, we suggest *Juanito's Centro Vasco.* Juan Siazortitria showed us how they make "Black Bean Soup" along with their "Arroz con Mariscos," which translates to "Rice with Shrimp," but as you'll see in the recipe, it's much, much more.

At The Forge, *dinner is beautifully served and doggie bags are "gift wrapped."*

Photo by the author

MANGO MORADA

Marker 88

2 large mangoes, peeled and diced
4 large scoops of vanilla ice cream
½ cup Hershey's chocolate sauce
2 oz. Grand Marnier
½ pt. heavy cream, whipped
½ cup almonds, sliced, blanched, and roasted

☐ Top each scoop of ice cream with some of the peeled and diced mangoes, add chocolate sauce, Grand Marnier, and almonds. Surround it with the heavy whipped cream. Serves 4.

ARTICHOKE HEARTS MONTE CARLO

The Forge

1 cup lump crab meat
2 cups watercress leaves
¼ cup chives, chopped
2 T. parsley, chopped
1 clove garlic, minced
3 anchovy filets, chopped
1 cup mayonnaise
3 T. lemon juice
½ tsp. salt
¼ tsp. black pepper, freshly ground
½ cup sour cream
3 T. dill, chopped
12 canned artichoke hearts, drained
1 head bibb lettuce
pimiento and asparagus, for garnish

☐ Shred the crab meat with a fork in a small bowl. Combine all the remaining ingredients, except for the artichoke hearts and lettuce, in a blender until smooth and creamy.

Add half of the sauce to the crab meat and toss well. Trim the bottom of the artichoke hearts so that they will sit evenly on the plate. Take out some of the center leaves to form a cup. Fill each heart with crab meat. Place 2 filled hearts on beds of lettuce on individual plates and cover with the remaining sauce. Garnish with watercress.

Optional garnish: Decorate the artichokes with small pimiento cut-outs or tiny strips. Surround with a few asparagus spears and cross 2 strips of pimiento over each spear.

Refrigerate for 30 minutes before serving. Serve with thin buttered slices of pumpernickel bread. Serves 6.

BLACK BEANS

Juanito's Centro Vasco

1 lb. dried black beans, washed and drained
6 cups water
1 green pepper, chopped
½ cup olive oil
2 tsp. salt
1 smoked ham bone (optional)
¼ cup wine vinegar
1 cup chopped onion
1 garlic clove, minced
4 bay leaves
¼ tsp. pepper
2 slices of bacon, minced
1 tsp. sugar
½ tsp. ground cumin
1 pinch oregano

☐ Cover beans with water, bring to boil, and boil for 2 minutes. Cover pan and let stand for 1 hour. Sauté chopped onion, green pepper, and garlic in olive oil for 5 minutes. Add to beans along with bay leaves, salt, pepper, ham bone, bacon, cumin, and oregano. Bring to boil and simmer, covered, for 2 hours, adding more water if necessary. Add wine vinegar and sugar. Serves 6–8.

YELLOWTAIL RANGOON

Marker 88

2 lb. filets of yellowtail; if not available, snapper, dolphin, grouper or similar white fish
1 tsp. Worcestershire sauce
2 tbsps. lemon juice
1 tsp. salt
¼ tsp. white pepper
2 tbsps. cinnamon & currant jelly
rangoon sauce (recipe below)
flour, as needed
egg, beaten with a little milk as needed (egg wash)
1 stick margarine, clarified (recipe below)

☐ Clarified margarine: To remove water from margarine, gently heat the margarine in a saucepan until it melts. Then skim water off the top, until only the clarified margarine remains in the pan.

Rangoon Sauce

6 T. butter
½ cup each of diced bananas, pineapple, papaya, and mango, chopped parsley and lemon juice.

☐ Season the boneless filets with Worcestershire sauce, lemon juice, salt and white pepper to taste. Dip the filets in flour, then in egg wash.

In a skillet, sauté the filets in clarified margarine on one side only. Finish cooking by placing the filets, browned side up, in a 450° F. oven for 8 to 10 minutes.

When the filets are done, remove them to a serving platter, discarding the margarine. Sprinkle filets with ground cinnamon and spread currant jelly over it.

In a skillet, quickly simmer the rangoon sauce, stir gently and cook the mixture "only" until it is heated through. Top each serving of fish with some of the rangoon sauce. Serves 4.

CONCH BISQUE

Marker 88

8–12 oz. conch meat, cleaned and peeled (see note)
2 T. salt
4 T. flour
2 T. butter, melted
½ cup heavy cream
sherry
1 celery stalk
1 leek
3 sprigs fresh parsley
1 large piece fresh ginger, halved lengthwise

Note: If conch is not available, any ground, edible whelk (scungilli) or chopped clams can be used instead.

☐ Tie the celery, leek, parsley and ginger together with string for bouquet garni.

Grind the cleaned conch once in a meat grinder using a medium blade. Put the ground conch in a large pot with 2 quarts cold water, bouquet garni, and salt. Bring to a boil and simmer the mixture for 1½ hours. Remove and discard the bouquet garni. Strain the soup to remove the conch and set the meat aside.

In another saucepan, make a roux from the flour and butter. (The amount of roux may be varied according to the desired thickness of the bisque.) Add the strained soup, a little at a time. Stir constantly to eliminate any lumps, until all the liquid has been added. Return the conch meat to the pot.

Bring the bisque to a second boil and simmer for another 15 minutes. Add the heavy cream and heat just to the boiling point. Serve hot, with sherry on the side to be added according to taste. Serves 6.

ARROZ CON MARISCOS

Juanito's Centro Vasco

1 lb. shrimp, peeled and deveined
1 lb. lobster tail, cut into 1-in, chunks (with shell)
4 stone crab claws
8 clams in the shell, or fresh mussels in the shell
8 oz. snapper, cut into small pieces
8 oz. scallops
1 cup white wine (demi-sec)
1½ cups tomato sauce
2½ cups fish stock or consommé
3 cups Valencia-style rice or other short grain rice
4 red pimientos
3 garlic cloves
1 cup onions, chopped
1 cup green peppers, chopped
¼ cup peas
1 cup olive oil
¼ T. saffron (see note)
laurel, pepper, cumin, and salt, to taste

☐ In an oven-proof deep dish or metal pan, sauté the onions, green peppers, garlic in olive oil until golden. Add the shrimp, lobster, clams or mussels, snapper, and scallops. Also add the white wine and, after a few minutes, add the tomato sauce and fish stock. When boiling action begins, add the rice, peas, and the condiments to taste, as well as the saffron. Let it boil for five minutes and then place in preheated 350° F. oven for approximately 20 minutes (making sure that the rice is sufficiently tender). In the meantime, briefly boil the stone crab and set aside for garnish.

After approximately 20 minutes take the pan out of the oven and garnish with the red peppers and stone crab. You may also use a few hard boiled egg wedges and parsley to garnish. Finally, spread the peas over the top. Serves 4–6.

Note: "Arroz con Mariscos" is an improved version of the paella and so the yellow color should be obtained from the powdered saffron. However, due to the occasional difficulty in obtaining saffron, any good yellow color used in bakeries may be used.

Don Shula, Dolphin coach, is a commanding field general.

MINNESOTA

Minnesota is called the "Land of 10,000 Lakes." Within the city limits of Minneapolis alone there are twenty-two. The lakes, and the parks surrounding them, give the downtown area a rural feeling that must have a calming effect on hectic business days. Across the river is the second of the twin cities, St. Paul.

The area had its beginnings as a fort to protect the fur trade, and was originally settled by pioneers of German and Irish heritage. Many Scandanavians eventually settled here, and undoubtedly had an influence in the naming of their football team, the Minnesota Vikings.

The Black Forest Inn in Minneapolis serves fine German fare. Locals rave about their specialty, onion rings. We've included a simple recipe to try at home.

Probably the best known Irish pub in Minneapolis is *Duff's*. This is not a fancy restaurant, it's a pub, and it's the best place to be in Minneapolis on St. Patrick's Day. But be ready for a party. Last St. Patty's day they sold over 110 gallons of "Irish Stew." Bob McNamara sent us a letter that didn't give the exact proportions, but said the cook uses lamb, carrots, onions, celery, peas, Irish (what else?) small potatoes, tomatoes, salt, pepper, garlic salt, oregano, and a beer base.

If you want to sample some Scandanavian dishes, then *La Tortue* (The Turtle) is for you. Tor Aasheim, a native of Oslo, Norway, and his wife Kristen, have renovated a warehouse for their fine restaurant. Tor is a graduate of the famous Cordon-Bleu cooking school. With the help of Chef Paul Laubignot, a native of France, they have sent us recipes for "Gravlax" (marinated salmon) and "Ertesuppe" (Scandanavian split pea soup).

Across the river in St. Paul, another renovated mansion resulted in an unusual restaurant—*Forepaugh's*. The renovation and conversion from home to restaurant is interesting; all rooms are different. Some go for this uniqueness of surroundings, but most go for the food. Dale Beckerman sent us what they call "Hotch Potch," a seafood melange that is quite a meal for four.

On the St. Paul side of the river is Andy's Italian pick, the *Venetian Inn*. Mama Vitale sent us her version of Bracciole. Thanks, Mama.

As with many stadiums, the Viking's home is not in Minneapolis or St. Paul, but out in the suburb of Bloomington. Nearby is a place called *Eddie Webster's*. Tom Webster now runs the place, and it's a great place to go before or after a Monday night game, or, anytime. They sent us a very "local" recipe, "Minnesota Wild Rice Soup."

Photo by ABC Sports

MINNESOTA

ERTESUPPE
(Scandinavian Yellow Split Pea Soup)

La Tortue

3 ham shanks
3 lb. yellow split peas
2 bay leaves

Place ham shanks, peas, and bay leaves in 2 gallons of water. Bring to boil then reduce to simmer.

1 lb. salt pork, diced or ground
2 lb. onion, diced medium
1 lb. celery, diced medium
6 oz. flour
salt and pepper, to taste

☐ Sauté salt pork until some of the fat is rendered. Add the onions and celery and cook until nearly tender. Add the flour to make roux. Cook 5 to 6 minutes. Add one gallon of liquid gradually, stirring until slightly thickened and smooth. Add peas and ham shank mixture. Simmer one hour until peas are soft. Pass through food mill and china cap. Adjust seasoning and consistency. Remove meat from ham shanks and use for garnish.

ONION RINGS
Black Forest Inn

2 jumbo yellow or Bermuda onions
½ lb. flour
6–7 eggs
1 lb. white bread or cracker crumbs
vegetable or peanut oil
salt and pepper, to taste

☐ Peel and slice onions into ¾ to 1-inch thick slices. Separate slices into rings.
Prepare in separate bowls: flour with salt and pepper mixed in 6–7 well-beaten eggs; white bread crumbs or cracker crumbs.
To apply breading on onion rings, coat rings with flour, then dip into eggs; then coat with flour again, then eggs, then dip in crumbs and press firmly.
Fry breaded rings in 2 inches of 375° F. vegetable oil or peanut oil.
Serves 9–14.

GRAVLAX
(Marinated Salmon)

La Tortue

3–4 lb. fresh Salmon
4 T. dill
1 tsp. white pepper
4 oz. cognac
2 oz. cooking sherry
1¼ oz. sugar
3¾ oz. salt

☐ Place salmon in pan large enough to hold it; be certain pan is not too large. Mix white pepper and salt. Spread sugar and salt-pepper mixture evenly over the salmon. Splash evenly with cognac and sherry until moist. Press with wooden or plastic board and leave for 12 to 14 hours. Once it has been sitting pressed in the refrigerator for this length of time, everything should be dissolved. If not, taste and use less the next time.
If you use a smaller salmon, use less of all ingredients and leave for less time. The salmon will keep in the refrigerator for up to two weeks if wrapped in waxed paper. Serve cold and thinly sliced, with "Mustard/Dill Sauce."

Mustard/Dill Sauce
10 T. prepared mustard
10 T. sugar
Plenty of dill, fresh or frozen
1 cup white vinegar

Mix together prepared mustard, sugar and dill. Add white vinegar slowly until the mixture is the consistency of cream dressing. Serve cold as sauce for "Gravlax."

HOTCH POTCH

Forepaugh's

4 6-oz. lobster tails
4 King Crab claws
8 jumbo scallops
4 cherrystone clams
½ lb. baby bay shrimp
2 green peppers
2 onions
½ lb. fresh mushrooms
saffron rice
salt and pepper, to taste

Saffron Rice

1 qt. chicken stock
1 pt. white rice
1 onion, finely diced
1 small clove fresh garlic
pinch saffron
¼ cup butter

□ Sauté the onion, garlic, and saffron together for about 3 minutes at medium heat. Add rice and stir till rice is covered with the butter. Add the stock and stir. Cover pan and bake in the oven till tender at 350°F.

Seafood

□ After starting rice in the oven, julienne strips of the onion and green pepper. Wash the mushrooms and slice thin. Mix the onion, green pepper and mushrooms together and set to the side. Split the lobster tails and pull loose from the shell. Poach the lobster, crab, clams, and scallops together. When the shell fish is almost cooked, add the bay shrimp.

Sauté the vegetables in a little butter till tender. Remove rice from oven and stir. Place the rice on the bottom of a serving platter. Arrange the shell fish all around the outside of the platter, put vegetables in the middle of the platter and top with the bay shrimp.

Serve with lemon and drawn butter . Serves 4.

BRACCIOLE

Venetian Inn

2 lb. round steak, sliced thin and pounded flat
1 qt. tomato sauce, canned or homemade
2 cups bread crumbs
8 oz. mozzarella cheese, shredded
3 T. Parmesan cheese
¼ cup vegetable oil
2 cloves garlic, minced or crushed
1 tsp. dried sweet basil
3 T. parsley, minced
¾ tsp. salt
1 tsp. pepper
1 T. onion, chopped

□ Mix bread crumbs with Parmesan cheese, garlic, onion, sweet basil, parsley, salt and pepper in a large bowl. Place oil in skillet and heat until sizzling. Add bread crumb mixture and brown, stirring so crumbs do not burn.

Spread round steak (4-in. x 6-in. pieces) flat and place layer of bread crumbs on meat. Sprinkle with shredded mozzarella cheese and tomato sauce. Roll filled steaks tightly and wrap with string. Brown bracciole in skillet turning frequently.

Place browned bracciole in baking pan and pour balance of tomato sauce over top. Cover and bake at 350° F. for 50 to 60 minutes or until tender. Remove bracciole from baking pan and cool to remove string.

To serve, slice bracciole and arrange on oven tray. Reheat in 300° F. oven until warm. Serve with a side of spaghetti and tossed Italian vegetable salad. Serves 4.

CREAM OF WILD RICE SOUP

Eddie Webster's

¼ cup diced celery
¼ cup diced onions
⅛ cup diced green peppers
2 large mushroom buttons, sliced
½ lb. butter
½ cup white flour
½ gal. chicken stock (water from one stewing chicken)
⅓ lb. wild rice
1 tsp. pimientos
1 oz. or less white wine
salt, pepper, sugar, MSG, pinch to taste
half & half

□ To make a successful Wild Rice Soup, you will need a very mild chicken stock. This can be obtained by taking one stewing chicken and boiling in ½ gallon of water. When you have achieved your stock, remove and discard chicken. You may want to add very hot water to thin. Keep hot until needed.

Next put approximately ⅓ lb. of wild rice in pan, covering rice with water, putting on a medium high heat until rice has cooked. Wild rice varies dramatically and, of course, we suggest you obtain the finest hulled rice. While cooking rice, add hot water; you should have ½ water and ½ rice when fully cooked. The water holds the flavor of the wild rice. Do not discard. It is as important as the rice itself.

Take butter, melt in frying pan; slowly bring heat up, being careful not to scorch the butter. Add celery, onions, green pepper, and mushroom, cooking ever so slightly. Next slowly add flour by sprinkling and stirring—you may add very hot water as needed to thin. Heat until a high gloss appears on roux. Next add your roux to the hot chicken stock, stirring until molded together. Next add wild rice and water, and stir until well mixed. Next add pimientos, wine, salt, pepper, sugar and MSG, to suit taste. Do not use cooking wine—a Chablis or Sauterne works best. Next add half and half to give richness .

NEW ENGLAND

Boston was foremost in protesting the tyranny of the British Crown, and in 1775 Paul Revere carried the call to arms that began the American Revolution. The name of the area's football team, the New England Patriots, reflects this heritage. New England fans are so aggressive that sometimes we've thought there was another revolution in the stands. Had the British known anything about Boston crowds, they might never have shown for the "big match up" at Lexington and Concord.

One of the sites of American resistance to the British still preserved is the ship that was raided in the "Boston Tea Party." Not far from the ship, further down the Boston Pier, is some of the finest seafood to be had anywhere in the United States. This is lobster country.

Our "redcap," Bill Edwards, is the man who keeps in contact with the referees to make sure we're back from commercials before play is resumed after a time out. A man of many year's road experience, Bill prefers *Anthony's Pier 4.* This is probably the most famous of the seafood restaurants on the pier. Because it is so well known, it is a good idea to make reservations.

Jimmy's Harborside Restaurant, a few blocks further east on the pier (Northern Avenue), is the favorite of many locals. Jimmy Doulos shared his recipe for baked stuffed lobster with us, as well as a stuffed filet of sole with "Lobster Newburg" sauce. After dinner *we* were stuffed.

There are many more places for excellent seafood in this town, and depending on whom you ask, you'll get different opinions of which is best. One of the oldest, *Union Oyster House,* established in 1826, has been consistently good for over a century and a half. You feel the history of the area just walking up to the building. To show there is more than one way to stuff sole, and that every seafood house is not the same, we're printing the Union's recipe for baked stuffed sole as well. We'll let you decide which is best.

The New England Patriots play their games in Schaefer Stadium, which is in Foxboro, Massachusetts, quite a ride south of Boston. Patriots' fans from all over New England can boast fine seafood restaurants from their towns along the coast. In North Kingston, Rhode Island, is *Custi's.* The sea's bounty is all there for the taking, served on a seafood buffet that can make the heartiest of seafood lovers cry "uncle." To dine at a place like this, it's best to make it the only meal of the day, and cancel all appointments. They shared with us a local standard, "New England Clam Chowder."

Two New England standards, the clam bake and clam chowder, were introduced to the Colonials by the Indians. The original chowder recipe called for a cube of bear fat, but pork fat has since replaced it. A local version passed along by Billy Rappaport (one of the college students from Boston we employ as a "runner" or "gopher" during the event), follows.

Locals know they can depend on Jimmy's Harborside *for great seafood.*

JIMMY'S BAKED STUFFED FILLET OF SOLE WITH LOBSTER NEWBURG SAUCE

Jimmy's Harborside Restaurant

2 slices bread, trimmed, diced
1 T. cracker crumbs
½ lb. butter
2 oz. sherry
1 tsp. Parmesan cheese, grated
½ lb. lobster meat, cut in small pieces
2 T. flour
1 cup light cream
1 cup milk
4 slices sole filets (7–8 oz. per serving)
cracker crumbs

Stuffing

☐ Mix diced bread with cracker crumbs, 4 tablespoons melted butter, 1 ounce sherry, grated Parmesan cheese, and ¼ pound lobster meat.

Filets of Sole

☐ Roll filets of sole with stuffing as prepared above. Place them in a pan, brush lightly with butter and add ½ cup of milk to keep moist. Place in 350° F. oven and bake for 10 minutes.

White Sauce

☐ In a saucepan place 4 tablespoons melted butter, add 2 tablespoons flour and whip slowly. Add warm milk and cream, simmer until thickened.

Lobster Newburg Sauce

☐ Place in saucepan 1 tablespoon butter. Add remainder of lobster, sherry, and paprika. Saute ½ minute. Add white sauce and simmer for 5 minutes.

Pour Newburg Sauce over filets and bake for 5 minutes.

BAKED STUFFED LOBSTER

Jimmy's Harborside Restaurant

1–2 lbs. fresh lobster
2 oz. bread crumbs, freshly ground
⅛ lb. butter
1 tsp. Parmesan cheese, grated
2 oz. fresh crabmeat or Alaskan crabmeat

☐ Split lobster open and remove intestines. Boil the claws and then remove the meat. Combine claw meat, knucklemeat, crabmeat, and stuffing and mix thoroughly and place in the lobster shell. Spread bread crumbs and melted butter over top. Preheat oven to 400° F. Bake 20–25 minutes. Baste with more melted butter to keep moist.

BAKED STUFFED SOLE

Union Oyster House

1 8-oz. sole filet, per person
8 oz. mushrooms, sliced
1 small onion, diced
1 small bunch parsley, finely chopped
4 oz. scallops
4 oz. langostinos
4 oz. baby shrimp
6 oz. butter
1 2-oz. bag potato chips
8–12 oz. bread crumbs
Pepper to taste
2 small cloves garlic, finely chopped
sherry

☐ In a heavy bottom saucepan, place 4 ounces of butter. Sauté garlic and onion until transparent, add scallops, langostinos, shrimp. Cook until just done, add about 2 ounces sherry wine, cook 3–4 minutes more then add chips and crumbs until mixture holds together. Add about ½ cup of parsley. Stir together, let cool.

Take approximately 2–3 ounces of cool mix and place on top of sole filet and roll until all sole is stuffed. Place joined side down in a buttered baking dish or casserole. Cover with buttered brown or wax paper. Cook at 350° F. until done, approximately 12–18 minutes, then remove from oven. Take off paper. If prepared in a casserole, serve with the Newburg sauce

and garnish with chopped parsley. If prepared on large pan, remove to heated dish. Serve with Newburg sauce and garnish with chopped parsley.

Newburg Sauce

1½ qt. Half & Half cream, hot
8 oz. butter
4 oz. flour
4 oz. sherry
2 oz. shallots, finely chopped
½ lb. scallops, cut up fresh
½ lb. langostinos
½ lb. baby shrimp, cooked
½ oz. paprika
salt and pepper, to taste

In a pan place 3 ounces butter and shallots. Cook until transparent. Add paprika, scallops, langostinos, and shrimp. Cook until scallops are done. Add wine and reduce liquid to half. Add cream sauce.

Cream Sauce

Place butter in a pan; melt and add flour. Cook until bubbly. Add Half & Half. Whisk until thick. Season to taste. Cook after adding to seafood to incorporate flavors. Serve on sole filets.

Anthony's is probably the best known of the restaurants on Boston's pier.

NEW ORLEANS

A major port of entry, New Orleans is a city of contrast. Tradition, jazz, the Mardi Gras, a mixture of ethnic groups all living on ground so damp and sandy that houses have no basements, and even the cemeteries are tiered above ground. New Orleans was French in 1718, ceded to Spain 44 years later, and then French again by 1800. By the time the residents heard the news it had already been sold to the U.S. in the Louisiana Purchase. Through all of this the French and Spanish melded together into a single group, the Creoles, who have an ethnic identity all their own.

New Orleans is one of those cities that is difficult to cover in a single chapter. Entire books have been done on its many restaurants and unusual cuisine. Several restaurants even have their own cookbooks; we have included two such establishments in our own.

People often ask us, "What's the best restaurant in the U.S.?" This is a difficult question to answer, but "Breakfast at Brennan's" is hard to top. Owen and Maude Brennan opened *Brennan's* in its first location on Bourbon Street in 1945. Owen died shortly before the move to their present location on Royal Street in 1956. It is now run by Maude and her three sons, Pip, Ted, and Jimmy. The food came out a blend of French-Irish-Creole that could only happen in one place, New Orleans.

Brennan's has a cookbook of its own. Maude insisted it be small enough to fit in a coat pocket so that it's easy to take home. The recipes have been tailored so they can be prepared at home. The changes were made to save time for the home cook. The "Ramos Fizzes" are a must, but we must warn you. As tasty and seemingly harmless as they are, they'll get you if you let them.

Maylie's, established 1876, is just up the street from the Superdome, home of the New Orleans Saints. It is the oldest building on Poydras Street. William Maylie, grandson of the founder Bernard, has run the place since 1939, and the fourth generation is "waiting in the wings." This place is not fancy; in fact, you may drive past thinking you missed it, but once inside you'll be glad you stopped. Creole is definitely spoken here. William suggested we print the "Shellfish Gumbo" and the "Jambalaya" because they are famous Creole dishes that can be made with ingredients found anywhere. They sell their cookbook, with recipes that go all the way back to the 1870s, for a walloping dollar-fifty.

Tujague's is the second oldest restaurant, and oldest bar in New Orleans. Established in 1856, many things done here are still done as they were back then. Philip and Otis Gurchet have run it since the 1920s. Ron, Otis's son, was there when we stopped in. When we inquired about recipes, he brought out Brenda, the cook, and she wrote them out for us right there. Now that's service. The meals are reasonable to say the least. A five course lunch is $5.50. For a look at how it probably was 100 years ago in New Orleans, Tujague's should be checked out.

For a romantic evening of dining, may we suggest *Broussard's* or *Moran's*. Broussard's, located in the heart of the French Quarter, is a premier Creole, New Orleans-style place (jackets required for gentlemen). They offered us two entrees with an appetizer and a delicious strawberry dessert for publication. Thank you, Joe Segreto.

Moran's Riverside is another fine restaurant for a special evening. The service is magnificent and the food is the same. Their "Fettucine Alfredo" is prepared at the table, and the noodles are made fresh daily. Pecan wood fire is the secret of their very special "Rack of Lamb." These recipes were submitted along with a new menu item Jimmy Moran is quite proud of, "Crabmeat Dutch."

Le Chateaubriand is a restaurant in the French Quarter that Dandy Don likes. For the "Filet Stephanie" recipe, see Part II under Don & Susan's favorites.

We'd like to take the time to wish "Bum" Phillips and the New Orleans Saints the greatest success in the coming years. (If the Saints become a Superbowl contender, why, we'd probably *have* to come to New Orleans more than once a year.)

Photo courtesy of The Greater New Orleans Tourist and Convention Commission

BROILED BRISKET OF BEEF

Tujague's

1 3-lb. beef brisket
1 whole onion
2–3 carrots, sliced
1 bay leaf
salt, to taste
6 oz. Tabasco sauce
6 oz. Lea & Perrins sauce
6 oz. horseradish
12 oz. catsup

☐   Combine beef brisket with onion, sliced carrots, bay leaf, and 3 ounces of Lea & Perrins sauce, along with a healthy dash of Tabasco sauce. Broil 2½ hours and then slice the beef. On the side, serve "Creolee," sauce made from 1 bottle catsup, ½ bottle Lea & Perrins sauce, and 4–5 tablespoons of horseradish. Serves 6.

REMOULADE SAUCE

Broussard's Restaurant

1 pt. mayonnaise
2 green onions, finely cut
1 T. horseradish
¼ cup Creole mustard
2 T. parsley, chopped
juice of half a lemon
1 garlic clove, finely minced

☐   In a mixing bowl, add all ingredients for sauce, stir well with wire whip. Let stand at least an hour before serving. Serves 6.

BANANAS FOSTER

Brennan's

4 T. butter
1 cup brown sugar
½ tsp. cinnamon
4 T. banana liqueur
4 bananas, cut in half lengthwise, then halved
¼ cup rum
4 scoops vanilla ice cream

☐   Melt the butter over an alcohol burner in a flambé pan or attractive skillet. Add the sugar, cinnamon, and banana liqueur and stir to mix. Heat for a few minutes, then place the halved bananas in the sauce and sauté until soft and slightly browned.

Add the rum and allow it to heat well, then tip the pan so that the flame from the burner causes the sauce to light. Allow the sauce to flame until it dies out, tipping the pan with a circular motion to prolong the flaming. Serve over vanilla ice cream. First lift the bananas carefully out of the pan and place four pieces over each portion of ice cream, then spoon the hot sauce from the pan over the top. Serves 4.

FETTUCINE ALFREDO

Moran's Riverside

1 lb. homemade noodles
¼ lb. butter, at room temperature
¼ lb. Parmesan cheese, grated
2 oz. heavy cream, warm
fresh ground pepper

☐   Place a 6-quart pot, or larger, with approximately 1 gallon of water on burner at the highest heat. Add to water ¾ teaspoon of salt. When the water is boiling actively, add noodles, loosening and separating continuously with a long-handled fork. Over the pot, place the pan or bowl that you will mix the pasta in. When the pasta is cooked to your liking, drain about 98% of the water.

Place the noodles in the preheated pan along with the butter. Stir gently until the butter is melted, adding one-half the cheese and one-half the cream. Continuing to mix, add the remainder of cheese, and if more moisture is needed, add the rest of the cream. Stir a few seconds and serve. Add fresh ground pepper to taste. Serves 4.

CREPES BARBARA

Brennan's

2 lb. lump crabmeat
1 lb. boiled shrimp, cut up if large
¼ cup butter
¾ tsp. salt
¼ tsp. white pepper
8 T. Parmesan cheese, grated

Lemon Butter Sauce

½ cup brown sauce (rich beef stock and flour
    cooked together to a medium-thick consistency)
2 T. lemon juice
1½ lb. butter, melted
8 7- or 8-in. main dish crepes

☐ To sauté the crabmeat, melt the butter over low heat in a heavy skillet; then add the crabmeat and sprinkle with the salt and pepper. Stir very gently and cook over low heat just until the crabmeat is warmed through, about 5 minutes. Add the shrimp and set the skillet in a 175° F. oven to keep warm while you prepare the lemon butter sauce. Combine the ingredients for the lemon butter sauce in a small heavy saucepan and cook, stirring, over low heat until well blended. Set the saucepan in the oven along with the crabmeat. If you are using crepes prepared in advance and frozen, remove eight of them from the freezer and set on the kitchen counter to defrost while you prepare the hollandaise sauce. Also begin preheating the broiler for glazing the crepes.

To assemble the crepes, fill the center of each one with one-eighth of the crabmeat and shrimp, then top with one-eighth of the lemon butter sauce. Roll up the crepes and place them on a lightly buttered heavy baking sheet or cookie pan.

Spoon about 3 to 4 tablespoons of the hollandaise sauce over each crepe and place the pan under the broiler for a minute or so, just long enough for the hollandaise to begin to brown a bit. Remove the pan from the broiler and carefully lift the crepes, sauce and all, onto preheated dinner plates for serving. If you wish, spoon any sauce which remains on the baking sheet decoratively around the crepes. Sprinkle 1 tablespoon Parmesan cheese over top of each crepe. Serves 8.

SAUCE FOR STRAWBERRIES

Broussard's Restaurant

8 oz. cream cheese
¾ cup confectioner's sugar
2 T. vanilla
1 cup Half & Half

☐ Put cream cheese and sugar in mixing bowl, cream together; add Half & Half and vanilla, mix thoroughly. Let stand at least 30 minutes before serving. Serves 6.

Photo courtesy of The Greater New Orleans Tourist and Convention Commission

The French heritage of New Orleans lends a distinct flavor to the city's architecture.

JAMBALAYA

Maylie's

1½ cups Louisiana rice
1 T. butter
1 slice raw fat ham or ham fat
1 doz. chaurice (hot pork sausages)
1 cup shrimp, boiled
1 onion, minced
2 Creole tomatoes
1 sweet green pepper
1 sprig of thyme
1 bay leaf
2 cloves
1 T. garlic and parsley, minced
1½ qt. ea. beef stock and water
salt and pepper, to taste
cayenne, if desired very hot

☐ Cut ham into small pieces. Fry ham, shrimp, and chaurice in butter. Add onion and green pepper, then tomatoes. Add herbs and garlic and parsley, then hot beef stock and water, salt and pepper and boil a few minutes. Add rice which has been carefully washed. Cayenne may be added. Cook until rice is done or swelled, but not mushy. Serve hot.

Jackson Square was once called the Place d'Armes, *the heart of the French Quarter. Behind the statue of Andrew Jackson is Cathedral St. Louis, where the city gathered for Thanksgiving after the Battle of New Orleans.*

Photo by Jim Naughton

CRABMEAT "DUTCH"

Moran's Riverside

4 Creole tomatoes
1 lb. fresh lump crabmeat
4 leaves fresh basil, finely chopped
2 T. Parmesan cheese
1 fresh lemon
pinch fresh or dry thyme
1 T. parsley, chopped

☐ In a bowl, slice tomatoes medium thickness. Add pinch of thyme and basil, salt and pepper to taste; at the same time add Parmesan, mixing gently so as not to break up tomato slices.

Squeeze fresh lemon over mixture, and let rest for a minute or so. Go through the lump crabmeat gently to check for shells.

On chilled dishes, place tomatoes leaving just the natural sauce in the bowl. Now place crabmeat in the bowl along with the parsley and fold in the sauce. Place crabmeat over the tomatoes, using all the sauce over the dish. Garnish with a sprig of parsley, and a wedge of lemon. Serves 4.

RACK OF LAMB

Moran's Restaurant

☐ To prepare to cook, the lamb rack should be skinned to the layer of fat just next to the meat. The chime bone should be cut away to ease the carving. (The chime bone is the back bone and connecting parts to the rib rack.)

Rub the rack with salt and pepper, preparing to charcoal and smoke. Light the pit with about 5 pounds of coal. Let the fire burn until all the flames are gone, and the coals have a glowing ember.

Place racks on pit, and at the same time add pecan chips, which have been soaking in water. If you have a cover for your pit, close and just leave a little crack to allow the smoke through. Let the cooking and smoking process continue while you turn, as lamb browns and is smoked.

Rare: 20–25 minutes; medium: 25–30 minutes; well: 35+ minutes.

The pecan wood adds a flavor totally unlike hickory or any other wood.

EGGS À LA NOUVELLE ORLEANS

Brennan's

1 lb. butter
1½ lb. lump crabmeat
16 poached eggs

Brandy Cream Sauce

1 cup butter
1¼ cups flour
5 cups milk, hot
¾ tsp. salt
¼ tsp. black pepper
1 oz. brandy

☐ Melt the butter in a sauté pan or skillet over low heat. Add the crabmeat and cook slowly, stirring very gently, just until hot, about 5–8 minutes.

To prepare the brandy cream sauce, melt the butter over low heat in a saucepan. Stir in the flour gradually, cook for about 3 minutes, then gradually pour in the milk; continue stirring. Cook over low heat until the sauce thickens, then add the salt, pepper and brandy. Continue to cook about 5 minutes or until the sauce is medium thick.

To poach the eggs, bring the water and vinegar to a boil in a large skillet or sauté pan. Keeping the water at a continuous low rolling boil, crack the eggs, one by one, into it. Cook until the egg whites are firm, about 2 minutes. Lift the poached eggs out of the water with a skimmer or slotted spoon, allowing the water to drain back into the pan. Place them on a heated platter while you assemble the dishes. Place 3 ounces of lump crabmeat on each of 8 heated plates, then place 2 poached eggs side by side on the crabmeat. Ladle sauce evenly over the portions. Serves 8.

EGGS SARDOU

Brennan's

1 cup butter
1½ cups white onion, chopped
1¼ cups flour
4 cups milk
1 tsp. salt
½ tsp. black pepper
8 cups cooked spinach, chopped
16 large cooked artichoke bottoms, heated
16 poached eggs
hollandaise sauce

☐ To prepare the creamed spinach, melt the butter over low heat in a heated saucepan. Add the chopped onion and cook until just soft. Add the flour gradually, stirring constantly. Stir in the milk, still stirring, and cook until evenly blended and warmed through. Add the salt, pepper, and spinach and cook a few minutes more, just until the spinach is warmed through and the mixture evenly blended.

Put equal amounts of creamed spinach on 8 heated plates, then place two poached eggs and two artichoke bottoms on top of the spinach. Prepare the hollandaise sauce, then ladle an even coating of hollandaise over each portion.

Hollandaise Sauce

8 large egg yolks
4 Tbsp. lemon juice
1½ lb. hot melted butter, clarified
1 tsp. salt
¼ tsp. cayenne

☐ Put the egg yolks and lemon juice in a mixing bowl. Place the bowl over or near the pilot on top of the stove. Beat briefly with a whisk, then slowly pour in hot melted butter, beating briskly and constantly as you pour. When the sauce begins to thicken, sprinkle in the salt and pepper. Continue to beat while adding the rest of the butter. Beat until the sauce reaches an attractive consistency. When the sauce is finished, leave the bowl over the pilot or in a basin of hot water to keep warm until serving.

SALAD DRESSING

Broussard's Restaurant

¼ cup onion, finely chopped
1 pt. vegetable oil
2 eggs
⅓ cup white vinegar
1 tsp. sugar
1 T. white pepper
1 T. salt
1 T. chives

☐ Put all ingredients except chives in blender. Blend five minutes. Pour into mixing bowl, add chives and stir with whip. Let stand at least thirty minutes before serving. Serves 8.

CHEF MIKE ROUSSEL'S OYSTER LOAF

Brennan's

1 medium-size loaf French bread, or ½ large loaf, sliced across
1 T. butter
1 T. mayonnaise
½ T. garlic, finely chopped
¼ cup lettuce, chopped
Tabasco sauce
½ tomato, sliced
1 dill pickle, sliced, cut into several slivers
1 dozen deep-fried oysters (directions below)
4–5 very thin slices fresh lemon
corn meal
cayenne or seasoned salt
vegetable oil, for frying

☐ Butter both the inner sides of the French bread, then put mayonnaise, garlic, lettuce, Tabasco, tomato, pickle, and oysters on the bottom half in the order listed above. Cover with the top piece of French bread, then place in a 400° F. oven until crisp, about 3–5 minutes.

Oysters

To fry the oysters, drain them well, then roll in corn meal seasoned with salt, pepper, and cayenne— or use seasoned salt if you prefer. Fry in vegetable oil in a deep fryer heated to 375° F. for about 3 minutes per batch, or until golden brown and crisp; then drain on paper towels for a few minutes.

A bit of Mardi Gras hoopla.

NEW ORLEANS

The Farmer's Market in the French Quarter provides fresh ingredients for New Orleans' famous cuisine.

Photo by Jim Naughton

CHICKEN BONNE FEMME

Tujague's

2 lb. whole chicken fryer
3–4 potatoes, unpeeled
salt and pepper
1 clove garlic
parsley
oil, for frying

☐ In a large frying pan, heat cooking grease or oil to cover pan. Cut up fryer and add to pan. Season to taste. Cut potatoes like home fries and add to same pan when chicken is about half done. When potatoes are done, add finely chopped raw garlic and parsley. Mix everything together and serve. Serves 4.

VEAL OSCAR

Broussard's Restaurant

6 5-oz. veal cutlets from top round
1 lb. lump crabmeat
8 fresh mushrooms, sliced
12 jumbo green asparagus
1 pt. hollandaise sauce

☐ Cook asparagus in salt water, let cool. Sauté mushrooms in four ounces of butter and add crabmeat. Toss for three or four minutes. Dust veal cutlets in flour, sauté until done. Put on six plates with two asparagus, one on each side. Cover veal with crabmeat and top with hollandaise sauce. Glaze under broiler. Serve at once. Serves 6.

80

SHELLFISH GUMBO

Maylie's

1 doz. hard-shelled crabs, or equivalent fresh crab-
    meat
1 lb. lake shrimp
1 doz. oysters
1 onion, chopped
3 large Creole tomatoes
2 qt. fresh okra
1 sprig thyme
1 T. garlic and parsley, minced
2 T. lard
salt and pepper, to taste
2 green peppers

☐ If crabs with shells are used, be sure they are alive. Scale and clean crabs, "taking off the dead man's fingers and sandbags." Shell shrimp and remove sand veins. Remove all pieces of loose shells from oysters. Heat lard and drop in onion and okra that has been cut into small pieces. Do not use the large ones with big seeds unless they are very tender. Let smother before adding seeded tomatoes and other seasonings. Fry crabs and shrimp and add okra, which must be stirred occasionally. Add oyster water and 3 quarts hot water. Oyster should be inserted only 15 or 20 minutes before serving. Let simmer for about three-quarters of an hour. Served with boiled Louisana rice. Serves 6–8.

SHRIMP ERNIE

Broussard's Restaurant

1 lb. shrimp (approx. 15–20)
egg wash (2 cups milk, 4 eggs)
1 cup yellow corn flour
vegetable oil, for frying

☐ Clean shrimp, retaining fantails; split and devein. Season yellow corn flour with salt and pepper. Dip shrimp in egg wash and roll in corn flour. Drop in vegetable oil at 325°F. and cook 5 minutes. Serves 4.

RAMOS GIN FIZZ

Brennan's

6 oz. gin
1½ oz. lemon juice
1½ oz. syrup (¼ cup sugar and 1 cup hot water,
    mixed until all the sugar melts)
2 large egg whites
½ tsp. orange flower water
1½ cups heavy cream
1 cup crushed ice

☐ Combine all the ingredients in a blender. Turn the blender on high speed for about 30 seconds, then off again, until the mixture is frothy. Serves 4 in old fashioned glasses.

TROUT LOUIS PHILIPPE

Broussard's Restaurant

6 8–10 oz. trout filets
1 lb. backfin lump crabmeat
1½ lb. butter
juice of 6 lemons
2 T. parsley, chopped
1 dash Lea & Perrins sauce
salt and pepper, to taste
2 eggs
½ cup milk
1 lb. shrimp (approx. 15–20)

☐ Melt 4 ounces of butter in sauté pan. Beat two eggs in cup with ½ cup milk. Dip trout filets in mixture and dust in flour. Put filets in warm sauté pan. Brown on each side and turn. When brown, place on warm platter. Melt 4 ounces of butter in two different pans. Put crabmeat in one and peeled, deveined shrimp in the other. Sauté each about 5–6 minutes. Add juice of one lemon to each. Place crab on filets, then add shrimp. Melt ¾ pound butter in saucepan. Brown and add parsley, lemon juice, and Lea & Perrins sauce. Spoon over trout and serve. Serves 6.

NEW YORK NEW JERSEY

New York, New York, the town so nice they named it twice. A town so big, there are two football teams, the Giants and the Jets. Today a parking ticket costs more than the $24 worth of trinkets the Dutch traded the Indians for the island of Manhattan.

The New York Giants, now sometimes called the "Jersey Giants," moved across the Hudson River several years ago to New Jersey. As proof to New Yorkers that there is life west of the Hudson, we're including a recipe from the *Mediterranean Armenian Restaurant* in Fort Lee, N.J. We chose the restaurant for its food, service, and its proximity to the Meadowlands, home of Giants Stadium; it also shows that in the New York area, almost every ethnic group is represented in a restaurant guide. Also in New Jersey is Andy's Italian pick, *Archer's.* You know the food has to be good if he chooses this one, considering New York City has its own "Little Italy." And considering that Archer's isn't an Italian restaurant. Their "Calamare (Squid) Salad," and "Fettucini Filete Pomador" (Fettucini with Pomador tomatoes), however, are fantastically Italian. Another favorite entree of ours from their wide range of continental cuisine is their rack of lamb.

In Manhattan, *Tre Amici* is another fine Italian restaurant run by some friends of ours. It is said that in New York you could eat in a different restaurant every day of your life and never repeat a stop. Needless to say, we had a hard time narrowing the field. So we've included some of our favorite places where we can always find a friend in front of or behind the counter.

When all five of our weekly workdays are not spent covering "the constant variety of sport," we spend our time at the ABC studios in New York. On Manhattan's West Side you can find the home studios of *Ryan's Hope, All My Children, One Life To Live, 20/20, and World News Tonight.* There are a few places close to the studios we frequent for lunch or an occasional cocktail or two after work.

Miss Penny from *Chipp's* has served us many a cocktail as well as many a Penny's Special, the recipe for which follows. Thanks, Penny. (We wonder how many times we've said "Thanks, Penny" over the years!) Next door to *Chipp's* is *Dimitri's.* It's more restaurant than bar, although there's always a little something going on at the bar here. The food is delicious, and the atmosphere is conducive to meeting someone for lunch. Two favorite entrees, "Steamed Bass," and tasty "Linguine Seafood Verde" follow.

This chapter would be incomplete without a New York deli, and *Zabar's* is the epitome of delis. They have an extensive selection of everything: meat, cheese, coffees, breads, fish, appetizers, cooking utensils . . . everything. Picnic baskets featuring all sorts of things can be ordered for a nice afternoon in the park. You may decide to browse and select your own menu. Try to find something they don't have—it's not easy. They sent us a few recipes, including one for a deli standard, the Reuben sandwich.

As an ethnic food paradise, New York seems like just the city to promote a restaurant that serves American cuisine. In case you've been in the city a few days and you've had enough ethnic, the *Palm* and the *Palm Too* feature good ol' steak, lobster, and chops. There are other Palm restaurants around the U.S. in other major cities, and all are safe bets for excellent food.

Downtown, the *Old Homestead Steak House* is well known for its steaks. If you want to try a New York strip steak the way it's meant to be fixed, this is the place for you.

Zabar's is New York's favorite deli. They've got it all — from the ingredients to the pots to cook it to the plates to serve it.

Photo by the author

ARMENIAN WEDDING RICE PILAF

Mediterranean Armenian Restaurant

1 lb. ground lamb
6 T. butter
½ cup almonds, blanched
½ cup pistachio nuts; blanched and peeled
½ cup pine nuts, blanched
2 tsp. salt
½ tsp. black pepper
½ T. Armenian spices
2 cups rice
3 cups chicken broth

☐ Place ground lamb in frying pan and brown thoroughly with 2 tablespoons of butter. Add the next six ingredients, stirring constantly. Sauté for 5 minutes. Set aside.

Bring 3 cups of chicken broth to a boil with 4 tablespoons of butter. Add rice and 1 teaspoon salt. Simmer until tender.

Add meat and nut mixture to rice and simmer together for 15 minutes.

HOMEMADE ANTIPASTO SALAD

Zabar's

½ small head cauliflower
½ cup artichoke hearts
1 large onion, sliced
½ cup baby corn
½ cup hot green pepper (peperoncini)
½ cup carrot, sliced
½ cup celery, chopped
½ cup green olives
2 tsp. capers, drained
¼ cup red wine vinegar
¾ cup olive oil
1 clove garlic, crushed
¼ tsp. pepper

☐ Break cauliflower into small pieces. In a large bowl, combine them with other vegetables, olives, and capers (be sure everything is well drained).

Shake vinegar, olive oil, garlic, and pepper in a jar; pour over vegetables. Let marinate in refrigerator 48 hours before serving. Serves 4.

NEW YORK NEW JERSEY

SEAFOOD FRA DIAVOLO

Tre Amici

1 lb. linguini
8 clams
8 mussels
4 shrimp
1 cup olive oil
2 cloves of garlic
1 lb. #303 can of imported plum tomatoes
oregano to taste
basil to taste
salt & pepper to taste
crushed red pepper to taste

☐ Brown garlic in heated olive oil. Drain off excess water from canned tomatoes. Add tomatoes to oil, add seasoning, bring to boil, and then reduce heat and simmer for fifteen minutes. Then add clams, mussels, and shrimp and cook for five minutes.

In a pot of three quarts boiling salted water, add the linguini. Cook and stir for ten minutes to obtain "al dente." Drain off water in collander and place linguini on large platter. Place Diavolo sauce along with seafood on top of linguini and serve.

PENNY'S SPECIAL

Chipp's

1 loaf French or Italian bread
12 slices ham or salami
12 slices bacon, cooked until crisp
12 slices tomato
12 slices Muenster cheese
onions or hot peppers, if desired

☐ Cut bread in half lengthwise. Scoop out inside of bread and butter liberally. Place ham or salami or both on buttered bread and place in oven or broiler until ham is hot. Place tomato slices, then bacon, and ending with cheese on ham and place back in oven or broiler until cheese is melted. For those with a heartier appetite, chopped onions or hot peppers may be placed on buttered bread before other ingredients.

Cut into slices.

This sandwich can be prepared in advance and then put into oven or on grill (good for summer) until piping hot. Wrap in foil. Serves 1.

THE REUBEN SANDWICH

Zabar's

4 slices rye bread
2 T. unsalted butter or margarine
¼ cup Russian dressing
½ lb. corned beef, sliced
¼ lb. Swiss cheese, sliced
¼ lb. sauerkraut, well drained

☐ Preheat oven to 425° F.
Spread 2 slices of bread with butter or margarine,

2 with Russian Dressing. Layer corned beef, Swiss cheese, and sauerkraut on the dressing; top with other bread slices, butter side down. Wrap tightly in aluminum foil, and bake about 15 minutes, or until hot.

If you prefer, butter one side of all 4 bread slices. On unbuttered side of 2 slices, spread dressing and layer corned beef, cheese, and sauerkraut; top with other 2 bread slices, buttered side up. Sauté in a skillet, over medium heat, turning once, until bread is golden brown on both sides and cheese is melted. Makes 2 sandwiches.

LINGUINE SEAFOOD VERDE

Dimitri's

4 medium-size shrimp, diced
¼ lb. sea scallops, diced
8 clams, diced (save juice)
1 sprig ea. parsley, basil and spinach, finely
    chopped
2 oz. virgin olive oil
2 cloves garlic, chopped
crushed red pepper, to taste
pinch salt
2 oz. white wine
1 lb. linguine

☐ Cook pasta *al dente*.
Put olive oil and garlic in a sauté pan and heat. Put into same pan, shrimp, scallops, clams, parsley, basil, and spinach. Add white wine and clam juice. Bring all ingredients to a boil. Remove from flame and pour over cooked pasta. Serves 4.

STEAMED SEA BASS

Dimitri's

2½–3 lb. whole sea bass
6 slices fresh ginger
3 scallions, sliced julienne style
1 oz. soy bean oil
½ oz. sesame oil
2 cloves garlic, crushed
hot pepper, to taste
3 tsp. soy sauce
2 tsp. water
snow peas

☐ Take sea bass and score it. Put in cavity of fish 4 slices fresh ginger. Cook in salted water for 15 minutes. Remove and put on a platter.

Put into a saucepan 1 ounce soy bean oil, ½ ounce sesame oil and heat. Add garlic and hot pepper. Take scallions and put them on top of fish. Take oil and garlic mixture, along with 2 teaspoons soy sauce, and pour on fish.

Dress platter with snow peas prepared as follows: sauté in a hot pan with a little oil, 2 slices ginger, 1 clove garlic for 1 minute; then add 1 teaspoon soy sauce and 2 teaspoons water for 1 minute or longer. Arrange around fish. Serves 4.

OAKLAND
SAN FRANCISCO

Many people think of San Francisco as the most beautiful city in the U.S. and for good reason. There is a charm to the place. The steep hills, the Bay, the cable cars, Chinatown, the fog, and the ornately painted old buildings juxtaposed with the modern architecture, give it a unique personality. There are many fine restaurants. We have chosen two well-known and two newer, lesser known restaurants to represent the city where Tony Bennett left his heart.

Scoma's, down on Fisherman's Wharf, is one of the best known places in town. Locals may tell you there are other places as good on the wharf, and there may well be, but for good reason the place does great business. Their "Cioppino," and another version, their "Lazy Man's Cioppino," are two dishes that always bring us back. Either one is a meal and a half. The recipes for both follow, along with "Calamari alla Anna," a special dish, and "Shrimp or Crablegs Sauté Bordelaise."

Before or after dinner in San Francisco, a stroll down the wharf will prove most satisfying. To whet your appetite, you can try the various seafood cocktails made fresh on the wharf. Not too much time is spent between the fisherman's net and your mouth.

A traditional bread in San Francisco is sourdough. Made from fermented dough baked without yeast, the process dates back to biblical times. San Francisco sourdough as we know it today began with the Gold Rush. Some historians believe it may have come from Mexico along with Mexican tools and mining methods. Others think the French brought it.

Isadore Boudin established the French Bakery on Depot Street (now Grant Avenue) back in the Gold Rush days. The *Boudin Bakery* now bakes bread fresh daily on Fisherman's Wharf seven days a week. The recipe, although it contains only flour, salt, and water, is prepared with the original mother dough, and that is a closely guarded secret. If you live in any state excluding Utah, you can have the bread shipped (including Alaska and Hawaii). It's worth the effort. The bread is truly unique, truly delicious, and it will arrive fresh. (The address is in the appendix.)

A well-known restaurant to represent Chinatown is *Kan's*. The food and recipes from here are so enjoyed that Johnny Kan wrote his own cookbook entitled *Eight Immortal Flavors*. We were sent three recipes from the book. The "Buck Ging Ngow Yuke" ("Peking Beef") was another closely guarded secret until Chef Sun Pui Wong allowed it to be published.

A new San Francisco tradition is "Joe's Special" prepared at *MacArthur Park*. This place, along with *Ciao*, an Italian restaurant around the corner, is part of a new breed in the Bay area.

MacArthur Park is more of a place to meet people. Ciao is the better place of the two for dining. Bill Higgins, the director of operations and part of the "new breed" of restaurateurs in the Bay area, also happens to be a high school buddy of Gary's. Although we didn't get a chance to try another of their Italian restaurants, *Prego*, Bill assures us it's the same fine quality. Poor Bill had to spend months in Italy tasting recipes for the place. Well, as he said, someone's got to do it. Having spent many frustrating years in Chicago as a Bears fan, he was hard to quiet down about his new team, the World Champion San Francisco 49ers.

Across the Bay, only a year earlier, the Oakland Raiders were the World Champions. Jack London Square is the East Bay's tourist attraction and its dining capital. Jack London, who wrote *The Call of the Wild*, along with fifty other novels and over 200 short stories, grew up there. The story has it that he was an oyster pirate, and spent much time in *Heinold's First and Last Chance Saloon*, one of the few restaurants of London's past that is the same today. A fine seafood restaurant in the same area is named after another of London's novels, *The Sea Wolf*. The area, along with Jack London Village not too far away, is full of restaurants and shops.

A "sandwich and beer joint" we feel deserves mention is *Sam's Hofbrau* in Oakland. It's near the stadium and before or after games, it's a swell place to sit out the traffic or grab a sandwich and beer. They also have turkey drumsticks we're particularly fond of. Pickles, slaw, and sauerkraut are complimentary.

Jack London Square attracts visitors to the East Bay for its sights and its dining.

LAZY MAN'S CIOPPINO

Scoma's

Oil (enough to braise onion and garlic)
1 onion, chopped
4 cloves garlic, crushed
pinch oregano
4 bay leaves
1 #10 can ground tomato in purée
salt
sugar
12 prawns
12 oz. crabmeat
12 oz. shrimp meat
12 clams
1 lb. red snapper cubes
¼ cup sauterne

☐ In a saucepan, brown garlic in oil. Then add chopped onion, bay leaves, and oregano. Sauté until onion is tender. Add ground tomatoes purée. Season with salt and a little sugar.

Bring to a boil and simmer for one hour. Add water and sauterne if sauce is too thick.

After sauce is cooked, add all seafood ingredients. When clams open, cioppino is ready. Serves 4.

PEKING BEEF (Buck Ging Ngow Yuke)

Kan's

1 lb. flank steak, cut into 2-inch cubes (Pound each cube once with tenderizing mallet.)
In a mixing bowl, marinate beef with:
1 T. dark soy sauce
1 T. hoisin sauce
1 T. tomato catsup
1 tsp. Worcestershire sauce
1 T. rice wine or sherry
1 T. Tientsin preserved vegetables
2 T. cornstarch
2 T. water
1 T. sesame oil
2 T. vegetable oil
1 clove garlic, finely crushed

☐ Let stand for 2 hours.

In a preheated wok or skillet, place vegetable oil. Bring oil to sizzling point at high heat. Add marinated beef. Toss-cook gradually to brown beef until just half-cooked. Add ½ cup of shredded onion and continue to toss-cook for one minute. Add dark soy sauce and one teaspoon granulated sugar. Blend well. Serve hot. Serves 4.

CRAB LEGS SAUTÉ BORDELAISE
PRAWNS SAUTÉ BORDELAISE

Scoma's

⅛ cup butter, clarified
2 doz. cooked crab legs or 1 dozen peeled and deveined prawns
1 doz. mushrooms
2 cloves garlic, crushed
1 small onion, chopped
¼ cup white wine
2 T. tomato sauce
2 T. cream sauce
parsley, chopped
1 doz. mushrooms, chopped

☐ In a skillet, brown garlic in butter (if cooking prawns, add here). Add onion and mushrooms. Cook for two minutes. Add white wine, simmer for three minutes, add crab legs and sauces. Cook for another three minutes. Add more wine if too thick. Sprinkle with parsley and salt to taste. Serves 2.

MIXED GRILL ALLA MILANESE

Ciao

3 oz. pork loin
3 oz. Italian sausage
3 oz. top round
3 oz. whole chicken
4 oz. quail
1 bell pepper
½ onion
seasoning sauce
2 slices lemon
8 oz. Vegetables, such as tomatoes, zucchini, mushrooms

☐ Skewer 'em up—and grill 'em! Serve on 9-in. plate with 2 slices lemon garnish.

JOE'S SPECIAL

MacArthur Park

8 oz. ground beef
2 oz. mushrooms
1 oz. onion
¼ bunch spinach
3 eggs
1 tsp. garlic
salt and pepper
lettuce, tomato and sprouts for garnish

☐ Slice mushrooms and place in sauté pan with diced white onions and cut fresh spinach. Sauté for about three minutes. Place raw ground beef in sauté pan and continue to sauté until beef is browned. Add garlic, salt and pepper while sautéeing. Break three eggs into pan and continue to sauté until eggs bind all ingredients together. Serves 2.

SWEET AND SOUR WHOLE ROCK COD
(Teem Seen Shek-Bon)

Kan's

1 2½-lb. fresh rock cod, cleaned
½ cup sugar
½ cup vinegar
⅓ cup pineapple juice
¼ cup catsup
1 T. Worcestershire sauce
4 drops hot sauce
1 large bell pepper, sliced
2 fresh tomatoes, quartered
½ cup dried onion, sliced
5 tsp. cornstarch
vegetable oil

☐ With a sharp knife, make a few incisions on both sides of fish, ¼ inch deep so sauce can penetrate. Season with salt and pepper.

Bring oil to boiling point and add seasoned whole rock cod. In a preheated wok or skillet, place sugar, vinegar, pineapple juice, catsup, Worcestershire sauce, hot sauce. Bring to a boil and add bell pepper, tomatoes and onion. Stir gently at high heat and again bring to a boil. Add gradually 5 teaspoons cornstarch made into paste with 5 teaspoons water.

Continue cooking at medium-high heat, stirring mixture until sauce has thickened. Pour mixture over fish and serve immediately with steamed rice. Serves 3 or 4.

Photo by ABC Sports

San Francisco's Joe Montana: the man with the golden helmet and the golden arm.

Raise your hand if you think the food's great in the Bay area.

CALAMARI ALLA ANNA

Scoma's

10 medium-size squid
½ cup whipping cream
6 eggs
2 T. lemon juice
1 T. white wine
1 cup oil
flour
salt
pepper
parsley, chopped

☐ Cut squid lengthwise and flatten, taking off skin and inside part. Tenderize by machine or pound by hand. Dip in flour and in egg batter.

Heat oil to 450° F. in a frying pan. Fry five squid at a time until both sides turn brown. Remove from frying pan and drain the oil. With open flame, return squid to frying pan and add wine, whipping cream and lemon juice.

Cook for two minutes or until sauce turns creamy. Add pepper, chopped parsley, and salt to taste. Serve with pasta and vegetable. Serves 2.

CIOPPINO

Scoma's

1 #10 can solid pack tomato, ground
2 medium onions, chopped
¼ cup olive oil
⅛ cup sugar
1 T. oregano
6 bay leaves
1 T. garlic, chopped
¼ cup sauterne
1 large crab, washed and cracked
8 clams
8 prawns
½ lb. bay shrimp
¼ lb. crabmeat

☐ Brown garlic in olive oil. Add chopped onions, wine, bay leaves, and oregano. Cook for 10 minutes over low fire. Add ground tomatoes and sugar. Salt to taste. (Sugar is added to reduce acidity.)

Simmer for 20 minutes. If sauce gets too thick, add more wine. Add all fish ingredients. When the clams open, the cioppino is cooked. Serves 4.

PINEAPPLE CHICKEN SALAD
(Baw Law Gai See Sai Lud)

Kan's

2 white agar agar strips, cut into 3-in. lengths
½ cup whole eggs, beaten
1 cup fresh cucumber slices, cored and cut into 2-in.
    lengths, medium-thin slices
¾ cup carrots, shredded
1 cup crushed pineapple, drained
½ cup chicken meat, cooked and shredded
4 T. sesame seeds
1 cup soy sauce
1 cup vinegar
½ cup granulated sugar
1 cup sesame oil
2 T. dry mustard, mixed with water
4 T. water
3 T. smooth peanut butter

☐ Soak agar agar strips in warm water for half hour. Drain and squeeze out excess water. Set aside.

Pan fry eggs into thin sheets. When done, shred into ⅛-inch wide pieces. Set aside.

Prepare cucumber slices, carrots, pineapple and chicken meat. On a large serving platter, begin assembling the salad by lining the platter with the softened agar agar strips. For the next layer distribute the fried shredded egg, making sure to leave a margin so that the bottom layer shows. In the same fashion, in a smaller circle, arrange the cucumber slices over the egg layer; then add the chicken pieces, followed by the crushed pineapple, each layer smaller than the first, so that you end up with a cone shape. Last, sprinkle over evenly with the shredded carrots. Keep refrigerated until ready to serve.

Salad Dressing

☐ Lightly toast sesame seeds in skillet or wok. Blend together in medium mixing bowl until smooth: soy sauce, vinegar, sugar, sesame oil, mustard, water, peanut butter.

To serve, sprinkle sesame seeds over the center of the salad and spoon dressing over individual servings. Serves 4.

Fisherman's Wharf means a wide selection of restaurants serving seafood fresh from the water.

PHILADELPHIA

In 1682, William Penn founded the city of Philadelphia on the banks of the Delaware River. The city bloomed quickly, and soon became a leader in culture, economy and industry. It was the center of political activity against the British before and during the Revolutionary War, and was the capital of the country until the Federal Government moved to Washington in 1800.

Many of the buildings where the most respected people of 17th and 18th century America worked, prayed, and lived, are still standing. Independence National Historical Park, on Walnut Street, is a four-block area bursting with early American history. The Continental Congress met, the Declaration of Independence was signed, the Liberty Bell rang, and the Constitution was written.

After the Civil War, Samuel Bookbinder opened a small restaurant on Walnut Street not far from this historical area, and just around the corner from the site of William Penn's slate roof home. The dockside location on the Delaware River enabled Sam to get fresh fish, spices from schooners that docked, and fresh oysters, crabs, and clams from the Chesapeake Bay. Sam's wife, Sarah, used to ring a bell at noon to announce to the dock workers, ship captains, and merchants within earshot that the principal meal of the day was being served.

Today, over 100 years later, the bell still hangs in the entrance of *Old Original Bookbinder's.* "Bookie's," now a seven-dining-room, three-bar establishment with a staff of 185, takes up close to a city block of space. Collectors' items, old maps, letters, and artifacts from Philadelphia's rich history are on view inside. Tourists are drawn here not only for the history on the walls, but for the consistently good seafood, served ever since Sam and Sarah's days. The Taxins, Albert and Doris, along with son John, are the present owners. The two recipes we've included can be found along with many more Bookbinder's favorites in a cookbook available at the restaurant gift shop. It can be ordered by mail as well as by phoning the restaurant.

Our schedule is so hectic that sometimes the only Liberty Bell we see in Philly is the giant reproduction in centerfield at Veterans Memorial Stadium, home of the Philadelphia Eagles. On nights when we work past normal restaurant hours, or when it's 3 a.m. and we've just got to have an eggroll, we're glad there are places like *Ho Sai Gai.* Discovered by one of the crew down in Philly's Chinatown, Ho Sai Gai also happens to serve some of the best Chinese food in town. Open from 11 a.m.–5 a.m., they serve Peking, Shanghai, Szechuan, Hunan, Taiwan, Hong Kong, and many other regional foods. Mr. Andrew Wu, the proprietor, showed us how to make Shanghai noodles and "Bean Curd Homestyle." If you don't have a wok, a frying pan will do, but the wok method of cooking the food does seem to add something. Bean curd, if you've never tried it, may sound strange, but it is a delicious source of protein.

We've been known to frequent *Ralph's,* in the same part of town, for lunch. Ralph and company have always made us feel welcome. We usually get there after the luncheon rush is over. This is the best time for a place like Ralph's. Whoever is cooking has the time to make your favorite dish just the way you like it. A favorite of the crew is either the fresh mussels or clams sautéed in olive oil over a bed of linguine.

Away from "the neighborhood," not far from Bookbinder's, is *LaFamiglia.* Some say it is the best Italian restaurant in Philly. As in most places, the best justifiably costs a little more. Due to the restaurant's popularity, and to Mama and Papa Sena's desire to make you happy, reservations are requested.

If you're looking for something a little different, try a place called *Marrakesh.* Behind an unassuming door on a sidestreet downtown called South Leithgow is a place straight out of *The Maltese Falcon.* The food is Moroccan, and so is the decor. Brass circular tables set low to the ground are surrounded by cushions you can sink and snuggle into. It's the kind of place you can loosen a few buttons, and take off your shoes. Rolling up your sleeves is a good idea as well, because the only utensils used here for dining are your fingers. The various appetizers and entrees are either dipped in or pulled apart. There is no need for a knife and fork. It's the Moroccan version of "finger lickin' good".

Photos by Jim Conroy

SHANGHAI NOODLE

Ho Sai Gai Restaurant

½ lb. egg noodles or yat gau mein noodle
2 T. oil
1 cup beef, chicken, or shrimp, in small pieces
onion, bean sprouts, or broccoli
2 T. Hoisin sauce
½ T. salt
½ T. MSG

☐ Put the noodles in boiling water for a couple of minutes. Drain. Run through cold water so that they won't stick together.

Heat oil, add beef, or shrimp, or chicken meat to the wok. When the color of the meat turns, add vegetable of your choice (onion or bean sprout, or broccoli, sautéed together). Then add noodles seasoned with Hoisin Sauce, salt, and MSG. Mix well and serve. Serves 2.

SPAGHETTI ALLA CARBONARA

La Famiglia

1 lb. spaghetti
¼ lb. bacon
2 cups heavy cream
3 eggs
parsley
Parmesan cheese
ground hot pepper

☐ Cook spaghetti in pot until *al dente.* In a separate frying pan, sauté bacon (make sure bacon is chopped into fine pieces first). When bacon is cooked, add heavy cream. Cook until cream is completely melted. Add spaghetti to the cream, break 3 fresh eggs on top of spaghetti. Cook on a low flame and mix thoroughly. Add parsley and hot pepper to taste. When sauce begins to thicken, add Parmesan cheese and serve. Serves 6.

VEAL CAPRICCIOSA

Ralph's

6 slices veal tenders (½ lb.)
6 slices eggplant, ½-in. thick
12 slices mozzarella cheese, ⅛ in. thick
6 slices prosciutto, thinly sliced
2 oz. milk
4 eggs
2 T. grated cheese (Romano and Parmesan)
1 onion, finely diced
1 tsp. salt, to taste
½ tsp. black pepper
½ lb. flour
8 oz. olive oil
12 oz. tomatoes, well ground

☐ Fry finely diced onion in the oil until it turns brown. Add the ground tomatoes in medium-size pot. Add salt and pepper to taste. Let simmer for 45 minutes on medium flame, stir occasionally.

Dip the eggplant in flour, then in the well-beaten eggs and milk. Fry in oil until golden brown. Put on napkins to absorb excess oil. Dip the veal tenders in the flour and fry lightly on both sides in pan that will hold the 6 pieces of veal. Drain off excess oil and add enough tomatoes and onion mix to cover bottom of pan (½ inch thick.)

Put the veal slices on the mix separately. Put one slice Prosciutto on each, cover lightly with more tomato mix. Add a little grated cheese on each slice, making sure there is enough grated cheese left for another layer. Put the slices of eggplant on each slice of meat. Add grated cheese that is left on each slice. Cover lightly with tomato mix. Top off with 2 slices of mozzarella, then cover with remaining tomatoes.

Put in oven for 20 minutes at 400° F.
Serves 2 or 3.

IMPERIAL CRAB

Old Original Bookbinder's

¼ cup butter
¼ cup flour
1 cup milk
salt and pepper
¼ cup green pepper, diced
2 pimientos, diced
½ tsp. Worcestershire sauce
1 drop Tabasco sauce
2 T. parsley, minced
2 lb. crabmeat
2 egg yolks, well beaten

☐ Melt butter, add flour, and stir until smooth. Add milk and continue cooking over medium heat, stirring constantly, until thickened. Add the rest of the ingredients and mix well. Continue cooking until heated through, but do not boil. Put into 8 individual casseroles and brown under broiler.

Photo by Jim Conroy

BEAN CURD-HOMESTYLE

Ho Sai Gai Restaurant

4 pcs. bean curd
1 T. oil
1 clove garlic, crushed
scallions
2 cups beef or pork, in small pieces
mushrooms, Chinese cabbage, green peas, or bamboo shoots
2 T. soy sauce
½ tsp. MSG
½ tsp. sugar
pinch salt
1 tsp. Szechuan hot sauce, optional
cornstarch

☐ Cut bean curd into 4 slices. Deep fry for one minute. Drain.

Heat oil in wok. Add garlic, some scallion. When the fragrance comes out, add vegetable of your choice, or meat of your choice. Add a cup of water, soy sauce, MSG, sugar, pinch of salt. (Add 1 teaspoon of Szechuan hot sauce, if you like it hot.)

Simmer for 2 minutes. Thicken with solution of water and cornstarch. Serves 4–6 when served along with several other dishes.

VEAL NAPOLITANO

La Famiglia

6 pieces veal cutlet
3 cloves garlic, finely chopped
1 pinch oregano
3 fresh tomatoes, diced
½ cup olive oil

☐ Combine all ingredients in one frying pan. Pour in oil. Cover with lid. Cook until pan begins to boil, remove lid. Cook an additional 10 minutes and serve. Serves 2.

PITTSBURGH

This is Steeltown where, as Howard Cosell would say, "the Allegheny meets the Monongahela to form the mighty river known as the Ohio." Fort Pitt was built here in the early days of America for its strategic location at the meeting of the three rivers. A portion of the fort's wall still stands as a monument. Today, next to this wall, stands Three Rivers Stadium, a modern day fortress defended by the five-time world champion Pittsburgh Steelers. For a picturesque view of this junction, it's best to cross the Ohio and look back down from Mt. Washington on a street aptly called Grandview Avenue.

If you want the total experience, board the antique trolley at the trolley station at the bottom of the hill for the slow climb. Some residents still use it to commute up and down the hill. The ride is worth the time and the nominal fare.

There are a number of restaurants that take advantage of the view. One we have tried is *Le Mont*. The food, service, and view are excellent. Le Mont regularly receives the *Holiday Travel Magazine* Award for Dining Excellence. In 1979

Esquire magazine chose it as Pittsburgh's best.

The historic P.&L.E. Railroad terminal holds a magnificent 500-seat restaurant. This place doesn't just have a view of a landmark—it's in one! *The Grand Concourse*, a Chuck Muer restaurant (see Detroit), features "Charley's Chowder" as a specialty along with many other seafood dishes.

A friend introduced us to *Cornucopia*. If you don't mind food that tastes good and is good for you, you'll love this place. There are three "veggie" dishes to try.

We couldn't write about Pittsburgh without mentioning our friends the Verbanets. We've gotten many a "quick sandwich and a beer" at their place, *Al & Steve's 120 Bar* They've also cooked us a number of family-style dinners that have been appreciated away from home. Mary sent along her recipe for stuffed cabbage. The crew originally discovered the *120 Bar* because it's near the stadium. Federal Avenue is a few blocks north of where "the Allegheny and the Monongahela meet to form the mighty river known as the Ohio."

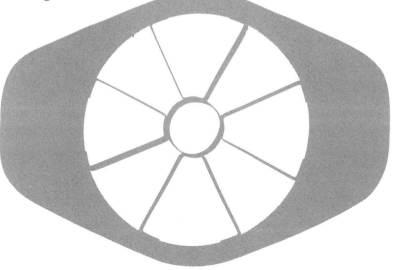

Photo by ABC Sports

PITTSBURGH

STUFFED CABBAGE

The 120 Bar

2 heads of cabbage
3 lb. ground meat
3 eggs
1 1-lb. can stewed tomatoes
4 tsp. Salt
3 cups rice, cooked
2 T. garlic powder
¼ T. pepper
¼ T. parsley
1 cup Italian bread crumbs
1 large onion, grated
6 stalks celery, chopped
1 11-oz. can sauerkraut
2 46-oz. cans tomato juice
4 lb. kielbassa

☐   In a large bowl, mix the following ingredients well: ground meat, eggs, stewed tomatoes, salt, rice, pepper, parsley, garlic powder, bread crumbs, onion, and celery.

Remove core of cabbage; place cabbage in large pot of boiling water, peeling off leaves as they become tender. Place leaf on board. Scoop the above ingredients on leaf, roll, tucking in sides.

Place sauerkraut and cabbage that cannot be used for stuffing in electric roaster, add tomato juice.

Stuff cabbage and lay on bed of sauerkraut and cabbage, add kielbassa and cook for about 3 hours or until tender at 350° F. Serves 12.

STUFFED LOIN OF VEAL

Le Mont

6 oz. Bel Paese cheese
10 oz. Prosciutto ham
1½ cups bread crumbs
2 cloves fresh garlic, pressed
½ cup fresh parsley, chopped
2 cups butter
1 24-oz. loin of veal
flour
Bercy sauce (a reduction of white wine and shallots added to a demi-glace; any basic brown sauce recipe will do.)

☐   Dice cheese and ham into medium pieces. Mix with bread crumbs, garlic, and parsley; add butter to keep it tightly together.

Separate veal loin from bone, cleaning away fat and skin. Slice loin lengthwise in half, open and pound lightly. Preheat oven to 350° F. Lay loin out and cover with stuffing mixture.

Slowly begin to roll veal and when finished rolling, tie stuffed veal together with butcher's string. Flour veal. Heat a sauté pan until it is very hot. Add a little butter to pan, then place stuffed veal in hot butter and sauté quickly on all sides to seal in juices.

Heat in preheated oven about 15 minutes to heat through. At this temperature, the veal should be medium to medium-well done. Serve with Bercy sauce (which has been strained through cheesecloth before pouring it over the veal), about two tablespoons finished sauce per serving. Serves 4.

LENTIL PATÉ

Cornucopia

2 cups red lentils, washed
1 cup red onion, minced
1 sweet red pepper, minced
½ cup parsley, chopped
4 cloves garlic, minced
¼ cup butter
4 eggs
½ cup Romano cheese, grated
½ tsp. black pepper
1 cup bread crumbs (whole wheat)

☐   Put lentils in a saucepan and just cover with water. Cook lentils on low heat until soft, about 45 minutes. Check after first 20 minutes to adjust water. Set aside to cool.

In a pan sauté garlic, onion, pepper and parsley. In a bowl mix eggs, Romano cheese, bread crumbs, and pepper. Mix lentil and garlic mixtures together and bake in a buttered 5 x 10-in. loaf pan for 1 hour at 375° F. Remove from pan then chill. Cut ¼-in. slices. Serve 2 slices on a bed of alfalfa sprouts with slices of avocado.

FRENCH ONION SOUP

Le Mont

½ lb. veal shank
½ lb. beef shank
2 gal. cold water
1 carrot, diced
2 celery stalks, diced
1 onion, diced
5 peppercorns
4 sprigs fresh parsley
1 clove garlic
24 small or medium-small onions, sliced very thin
¼ cup flour
salt
6 slices french bread, buttered and toasted
6 slices imported Gruyère cheese
2 T. Parmesan cheese, grated

☐ Place veal and beef shanks in water and bring to a fast boil. Boil 15 minutes, skimming occasionally. Add carrots, celery, diced onion (this mixture is called mirepoix), peppercorns, and herbs; simmer for another 1½ hours.

While broth is cooking, sauté sliced onions in butter until golden brown, placing them in another pot as they brown. Add flour to sautéed onions and toss over heat for 3 to 5 minutes so flour cooks out. Stir and set aside.

Strain stock and add to onion mixture. Cook 10 to 15 minutes. Add salt and adjust seasonings. Preheat oven to 325° F.

To serve, place the French bread slices in individual soup bowls and fill bowls with soup. Place a slice of Gruyère over top of each bowl, sealing it, and cover with a teaspoon of grated Parmesan. Bake in oven until cheese melts, about 5 to 10 minutes. Cheese should be lightly browned and bubbly. Serve immediately. Serves 6.

RATATOUILLE

Cornucopia

The first five ingredients should be diced in ½-inch pieces:

4 cups eggplant
4 cups zucchini
1 cup onions
1 cup sweet red peppers
2 cups tomatoes, peeled and seeded
1 T. dried sweet basil leaves
1 T. dried marjoram leaves
1 cup olive oil
10 cloves garlic, minced
½ cup brine-cured olives, pitted
salt and pepper, to taste

☐ Sauté separately eggplant, zucchini, onions, peppers. Then put them all together in a casserole.

Add tomatoes, herbs, and olives. Using a little of the left over oil, sauté the garlic until beige-colored. Add to the casserole and season with salt and pepper. Bake 45 minutes at 350° F. Serve with brown rice. Serves 4.

CUBAN BLACK BEAN SOUP

Cornucopia

2 cups black turtle beans
¼ cup parsley, minced
1 clove garlic, minced
1 large onion, minced
4 sweet red peppers, minced
8 cups water
1 T. marjoram leaves
1 T. whole cumin seeds
¼ cup olive oil
1 cup brown rice, cooked
1 tsp. salt
¼ cup white vinegar and lemon

☐ Soak beans overnight. Boil 1 hour. In another pot, heat the oil and add cumin seeds. Cook at high heat until seeds turn color slightly (about 1 minute). Add garlic and cook for 1 minute. Add onion and cook until clear (about 4 minutes). Add peppers and marjoram. Add boiled beans and salt. Cook until peppers are soft. Add vinegar, lemon and brown rice. Serves 4.

SPUMONI MOUSSE ALLA LE MONT

LeMont

¼ cup sultana raisins
½ T. maraschino liquor
3 egg yolks
½ cup fine sugar
½ cup sweet Marsala wine
¼ cup semi-sweet chocolate, grated
½ pt. heavy cream, whipped
¼ cup pecans, chopped
6 cherries

☐ Soak raisins in maraschino liquor 20 minutes. Prepare a zabaglione by combining egg yolks and sugar in top of double boiler above simmering—not boiling—water. Beat mixture with wire whisk until pale yellow and fluffy.

Gradually add Marsala wine and continue beating until zabaglione becomes thick enough to hold its shape in a spoon. Chill until it thickens a little more.

Fold in raisins together with maraschino liquor, chocolate, whipped cream and pecans. Pour mixture into 6 individual champagne glasses; chill 4 hours. Garnish each serving with a maraschino cherry. Serves 6.

Note: Zabaglione must be prepared slowly; allow at least ten minutes.

100

ST. LOUIS

St. Louis is known as the "Gateway to the West." Here, where the Missouri and Mississippi Rivers meet, was the last stop for pioneer families to get supplies before pushing west over the mountains to the Pacific. Steamboats paddled back and forth from New Orleans. In 1904 at the St. Louis Exposition, the hot dog and the ice cream cone were introduced.

The Gateway Arch, a 630-foot-tall steel arch, the tallest national monument, stands today on the river bank not far from several old steamboats that have become restaurants. The *Goldenrod Showboat,* now a national historic landmark, is moored there. The largest of its kind ever built, *Goldenrod* was the model for Edna Ferber's "Showboat." Ragtime concerts are given, galleries of pictures are on display, and a smorgasbord dinner is served.

If you want to get the riverboat feeling but forgo the entertainment, try the *Belle Angeline,* just down from the *Goldenrod.* The local fare is catfish and hush puppies, and midwestern hospitality. If you'd like the catfish but want to forgo the riverboat idea completely, you might try *Catfish and Crystal.* They also serve steaks and seafood for some variety.

Along with the history of St. Louis come a few of America's legends. Charles Lindbergh, supported by a group of St. Louis businessmen, made the first nonstop solo flight from New York to Paris in the *Spirit of St. Louis.* Legendary to the world of baseball were the "Gashouse Gang" and Stan "The Man" Musial. How is it baseball gets mentioned in a football cookbook? (Whoever heard of a football cookbook anyway?) St. Louis is the only city to have their professional baseball and football teams bearing the same name: Cardinals.

Stan the Man, and his friend Biggie, have a fine restaurant in midtown appropriately named *Stan Musial's and Biggie's.* It features steak and seafood. They sent two specialties of theirs, "Vinaigrette Dressing à la Musial," and "Chef Charlie's Chocolate Mousse."

A legend in the world of dining is *Tony's,* a five-star restaurant. Everything about this establishment is, as they say, "top shelf." The specialty is veal, but we asked them for some of their most unusual recipes. Try for instance their eggplant manicotti. Mmmmmm.

Andy's Italian selection, however, goes to *Kemoll's Restaurant.* This is taking nothing away from Tony's. Tony's is a five-star restaurant, and anyone could tell you it's good and be right. We've included Kemoll's because it also happens to be a fine restaurant, run by nice people, but is less well-known than Tony's. Frank and Ellen Cusamano sent us a recipe for chicken breasts, "Petto di Pollo Conti," that calls for dry vermouth, cream, and Prosciutto.

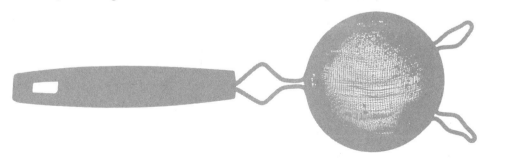

Busch Memorial Stadium hosts the St. Louis Cardinals — football and baseball.

Photo courtesy of The Convention and Visitors Bureau of Greater St. Louis

CAVATELLI BROCCOLI

Tony's

1 bunch fresh broccoli (flowers only)
1 lb. cavatelli
½ cup fresh mushrooms
½ cup fresh tomatoes, peeled and seeded
¼ cup Parmesan cheese
1 stick butter

☐ Boil broccoli in salt water. To this, add cavatelli; cook until *al dente*. Drain about ⅔ of the water off the pasta and broccoli, add sliced mushrooms, fresh tomatoes, grated Parmesan cheese, salt, pepper, and butter. Cook until blended together. Serves 4 as an appetizer.

EGGPLANT MANICOTTI

Tony's

2 eggplant
24 oz. fresh ricotta cheese
6 fresh tomatoes
fresh basil to taste
4–8 oz. heavy cream
1 cup olive oil
salt and pepper to taste

☐ Slice eggplant very thin; salt and let drain on towels for 35–45 minutes. Sauté in olive oil. Again, let drain to remove any excess olive oil. Season with salt and pepper. Spread eggplant with seasoned fresh ricotta cheese. Roll and bake in sauce made from fresh tomatoes, fresh basil and heavy cream. Serves 4.

VINAIGRETTE DRESSING À LA MUSIAL

Stan Musial's and Biggie's

Boston Bibb lettuce
Hearts of palm
Hearts of Artichoke
Jumbo Asparagus
Arrange vegetables on bed of lettuce.

Dressing

8 oz. oil
2 oz. red-wine vinegar
2 oz. cider vinegar
½ tsp. salt
¼ tsp. white pepper
1 T. sugar

Garnish

1 T. ripe olives, chopped
1 T. green olives, chopped
1 T. red pimientos, chopped
1 T. sour pickles, chopped
1 T. hard-boiled egg, chopped (white only)
1 T. chives, chopped
1 T. pepperincine (Italian peppers), chopped

☐ Mix dressing and add the chopped garnish to it. Arrange and serve on Bibb lettuce. Serves 8.

VEAL FRANCESCO

Kemoll's

2 medallions of Veal, floured and seasoned
butter, clarified
2 thin slices prosciutto
2 thin slices mozzarella
4 asparagus spears (top halves only)
¼ cup white wine
salt and pepper, to taste
1¾ T. tomato sauce
Parmesan cheese, grated

☐ Dip veal lightly in flour and sauté in clarified butter. Spread 1 tablespoon of tomato sauce on top, not too near edges. Place a slice of prosciutto on each medallion, spread ¾ tablespoon tomato sauce on top, not too near edges, then two asparague spears on each. Add the wine and simmer while scraping the bottom of the skillet. Top each of the medallions with a slice of mozzarella and lightly sprinkle with grated Parmesan. Cover the skillet until the cheese melts. Season to taste. Serves 2.

May be prepared ahead by undercooking veal, and placing in baking pan. Refrigerate and heat later (same day).

ZABAGLIONE

Tony's

8 egg yolks
8 oz. Marsala wine
8 tsp. sugar
vanilla
dash salt
24 whole fresh strawberries

☐ Put sugar in the top of a double boiler, add a few drops of vanilla, add wine. Stir until sugar is dissolved, add egg yolks and salt. Stir with wire whisk until eggs and wine become a creamy custard. Serve in a tall glass over strawberries. Sprinkle lightly with cinnamon.

Serve with wafers if you wish. Serves 4.

LOBSTER ALBANELLO

Tony's

2 lb. fresh lobster meat
1 lb. fresh mushrooms, sliced
6 shallots
4 oz. fish stock
1 qt. heavy cream
8 oz. dry white wine
butter

☐ Sauté the lobster meat and fresh mushrooms in the butter with the shallots. Add fish stock, heavy cream, and wine. Cook until sauce is blended well. Serves 4.

PETTO DI POLLO CONTI

Kemoll's

2 boneless breasts of chicken, seasoned in flour
butter, clarified
3 Italian green olives, cut into slivers
2 T. Prosciutto, cut into tiny pieces
⅓ cup cream
¾ oz. dry vermouth
salt and pepper, to taste

☐ Flatten chicken breasts. Dip lightly in flour and sauté in clarified butter. Add dry vermouth, reduce 30 seconds. Add olives and prosciutto, sauté for one minute. Pour the cream into the skillet with the chicken and the olives and reduce sauce to a medium heat. Season to taste. Serves 2.

CHEF CHARLIE'S CHOCOLATE MOUSSE

Stan Musial's and Biggie's

4 oz. German chocolate (semi-sweet)
2 egg whites
2 egg yolks
2 oz. granulated sugar
1 oz. white rum
1 oz. dark cream de cocoa
8 oz. heavy whipping cream
⅛ oz. cream of tartar

☐ Put German chocolate, cream de cocoa, white rum into a double boiler. Beat egg yolks, add to chocolate mixture. Cook till it thickens; let this cool.

Beat egg whites with cream of tartar. When very stiff, add sugar. Beat until you have a stiff meringue.

Whip heavy cream until stiff; fold above into whipped cream and meringue.

Put into your favorite stem glassware. Serves 4.

BIBB LETTUCE AND BELGIAN ENDIVE

Tony's

Bibb lettuce
Belgian endive
pure olive oil
red-wine vinegar
salt
fresh ground pepper

☐ Take the thinnest of Bibb lettuce and separate. Wash carefully; let drain several hours until dry. Separate endive leaves, using approximately twice as much Bibb lettuce as endive. Season lightly with salt and fresh ground pepper. Coat lightly with pure olive oil. Toss ever so lightly. Sprinkle a little red-wine vinegar and toss one time, again very lightly!

Serve on a chilled plate.

The beauty of this salad is it is elegant in its simplicity.

SAN DIEGO

ortuguese explorer Juan Rodriguez Cabrillo first discovered San Diego's natural harbor in 1542, claiming it for Spain. When Mexico won independence from Spain in 1821, California became a Mexican province.

The first American naval vessel sailed into San Diego bay in 1846, while California was still under the Mexican flag. Not long after, in settlement of the Mexican-American War, California became a part of the United States. Since then, San Diego has grown into a major American port and site of a U.S. Naval base. But it has never lost its Mexican flavor.

There is a picturesque view of the bay from the *Harbor House* in Seaport Village, a development of shops and restaurants just north of the Coronado Island bridge. From a booth by the windows you can see everything from sailboats to Navy vessels. "Butch" Bucciarelli, the owner, can be proud of his well-planned establishment. The different rooms include a bar and dance floor that are quite popular, two levels of dining, and an outdoor patio so San Diego's year-round good weather can be appreciated. Butch sent us the "how to" for one of our favorite entrees of the Harbor House, "Shark Embarcadero." Aside from the delicious flavor which is enhanced by the use of a mesquite wood fire for the broiling, we find something extremely satisfying about biting back a shark! The avocados on top of the dish make it really Californian.

There are many Mexican restaurants in San Diego. We recommend the *El Torito—La Fiesta Restaurants* for two reasons. The first is that restaurant "chains" get stereotyped because some people think if the same food is served in a number of places, it must not be good. We feel this is one chain that does not deserve that la-

bel. The food is very good, and the slushy Margaritas are "fantasticas." The second reason is they have a Monday Night Football Party every week there is a game, and we're behind anyone who watches the show and has a good time.

Speaking of football fans, not only is the "Church of Monday Night Football" in this area (hey, it's California), but so is an avid Charger fan who deserves mention. His name is John Wells, Jr., also known as "Johnie Cheesecake." John grew up in La Jolla and always was fond of cheesecake. While at school he learned from some of his Eastern classmates how "East Coast" cheesecake is made, liked it, and started making cakes as a sort of hobby. He was eating some cheesecake in a restaurant one day when he was heard to say he could make a better cheesecake. It was the proprietor, a friend of his, who heard the boast, and a wager soon followed. John brought in the cake, and you guessed it, he won the bet. The proprietor asked John to make a few a week for his place and the rest is history.

Hearing the Chargers' general manager describe the Charger football team as an "uncut cake with all the ingredients of a winner" set John's mind to thinking. As an incentive to the Chargers, John offers free cheesecake to the team after a victory. It costs him some cheesecake, but then the Chargers sure do win a lot.

John now supplies many restaurants in the area with both cheesecakes and quiches. The cheesecake recipe is a guarded secret, but he did send us a recipe for one of his quiches. Neither product is sold at stores, but if you'd like to try the "Best Cheescake in the West," you might dine at *Anthony's Fish Grotto* next time you're in San Diego. It has a family atmosphere, excellent seafood, and well you know about the dessert.

SAN DIEGO

Look at those smiles — we told you the Margaritas were good!

COQUILLE VERONIQUE

Anthony's Fish Grotto

Cream Sauce
Make 1½ cups of rich sauce and hold.

Lobster Stock
2 cups water
1 lobster shell, meat removed
2 bay leaves
1 celery stalk (top only)
1 small onion
salt, to taste

Simmer for 2 hours, then strain stock and hold.

Scallops
24 oz. scallops

⅓ cup butter
1½ cups cream sauce
1¼ cups lobster stock
2 T. sherry
1 tsp. salt
¼ cup each: Parmesan and cheddar, grated and mixed
20 large grapes, peeled and seeded

☐ Roll scallops in flour and salt and sauté in hot (but not burned) butter for 3–4 minutes. Mix cream sauce and lobster stock together and add. Now add sherry and grapes and sauté 2 minutes or longer, until piping hot.

Divide into separate serving shells, sprinkle lightly with cheese mixture and bake in 400° F. oven for 5 minutes. Serves 4–6.

CALIFORNIA QUICHE LORRAINE

Johnies Cheesecake, Inc.

½ cup diced ham
¼ cup Ortega green chili salsa
⅓ cup white onions
¼ cup mushrooms

Sauté in butter all of the above. Drain well.

4 Tbsp. flour
3 eggs, extra large
¼ cup California Solera Cocktail Sherry
¼ tsp. ground black pepper
¼ tsp. cayenne pepper
½ tsp. salt
1 tsp. Worcestershire sauce
1 cup milk

☐ Mix flour, sherry, pepper, salt and Worcestershire. Beat in eggs with whip. Add milk and mix well. Egg wash a 9″ deep-dish piecrust. Add drained sauteed mixture, spreading around bottom. Sprinkle over sauteed mixture:

¾ cup shredded Swiss cheese
¼ cup shredded sharp cheddar cheese
2 tsp. bacon bits
1 tsp. parsley

Gently pour liquid mixture up to edge of piecrust. Bake in pre-heated oven at 300° for 50 to 60 minutes.

SHARK EMBARCADERO

The Harbor House

4 8-oz. Thresher shark filets
6 oz. white wine sauce (see below)
8 oz. grated cheese (½ cheddar, ½ Monterey Jack)
2 slices avocado
2 slices tomato

White Wine Sauce

2 oz. shallots
3 oz. butter
2 oz. flour
2 oz. butter
¼ cup white wine
¼ cup clam juice
¼ cup whipping cream

☐ Sauté shallots in butter until light golden. Add flour and butter; heat and blend. Add wine. In separate saucepan, bring clam juice and whipping cream to boil. Then pour the liquid into the other ingredients and beat with a whisk for 3 minutes.

To prepare shark, broil over a natural mesquite wood fire. Sprinkle grated cheese over the filets, and melt under broiler or in oven. Pour white wine sauce over filets just before serving. Garnish with tomato and avocado.

CHILE CON CARNE

El Torito–La Fiesta

2 lb. ground beef, medium grind
2 tsp. salt
2 T. dark chile powder blend
1 T. chile Santa Maria
1 T. cumin
1 16-oz. can crushed tomato
2 bell peppers, chopped
1 onion, chopped
1 tsp. granulated garlic
2 cups enchilada sauce
1 celery stalk, chopped
1½ cups water

☐ Combine meat, crushed tomatoes, onion, peppers, celery, and water in a large roasting pan and place in 350° F. oven. Cook for one hour. Add all spices, cook for 3 hours. Every hour, skim all grease on surface of chile. In last hour of cooking add enchilada sauce. To cook on the stove, use 8-quart pan, cooking at high heat for the first hour. Cover pot and lower heat to simmer, add spices at the end of the second hour. Serves 6.

Photo by the author

San Diego's beautiful climate can be appreciated on El Torito's patio.

SEATTLE

This city began as a lumber camp, and was named after a friendly Indian who is credited with being one of the few in America to take the white man for a bundle of money. The legend has it that Sealth, or Chief Seattle, was approached by the settlers for permission to use his name for their town. Sealth contended that he would roll over in his grave every time his name was mentioned after his death, and that he should be paid for the inconvenience in advance. The settlers gathered approximately $16,000 for Chief Seattle, and the deal was made. If the Chief is turning over and over, we're sure he's smiling.

Blake Island, the birthplace of Chief Seattle, is located in the middle of the Puget Sound. This island was a meeting place for tribes of the North Coast native Americans. In the early 1960s, William S. Hewitt, a successful restaurateur and caterer from the area, tasted Pacific salmon prepared in the manner of the coastal Indians. The salmon is split, spread apart on cedar sticks, and baked before an alder fire. Mr. Hewitt was overwhelmed by the taste and aroma. With the help of others who wished to preserve the Indian culture, he made arrangements with the state of Washington to build a "longhouse" similar to those found in the villages of the area. The name was to be "Tillicum" which in Chinook, the local Indian tongue, means "people."

Today, those wishing to experience the culture of the local tribes can take a "Tillicum Tour" to Blake Island. There a feast is prepared featuring the salmon barbecue along with clams, clam nectar, salad, potato, and special Tillicum hot bread. After dinner, you can watch ceremonial dances, browse through exhibits of the Indian art, or take a walk on the nature trail. A blast of the whistle from the "Goodtimes," the ferryboat, signals your departure. The recipe sent for the "Barbecue Salmon" is definitely our most unusual.

It is hard to disassociate Seattle with salmon. In case you can't find a whole salmon to barbecue, or if open fires are against the code in your apartment, we've included "Salmon Wellington" along with "Red Snapper Duxelle" from *El-*

liott Bay Fish and Oyster Co. Elliott's is on Pier 56, the same pier from which the Tillicum Village ferry leaves. The restaurant features fresh seafood in a contemporary dining room with an atrium along the water. From here, you can see Seattle's waterfront and Elliott Bay.

There are so many good seafood restaurants here it's hard to mention just a few. The Ivar name is synonymous with good seafood. There are many locations in the area, *Ivar's Salmon House* on Lake Union, *Ivar's Captain's Table* on Elliott Avenue, or *Ivar's Acre of Clams* on Pier 54. We often stop at the Acre of Clams for a quick snack on the way to the Kingdome. They have clam chowder, fried clams, and clam nectar "to go"—all out of this world.

Fifteen minutes from downtown is *Stuart's* at Shilshole. Friends of ours from the area took us here for a fine dinner. There's dancing and cocktails in a comfortable atmosphere in the lounge.

In 1897, Seattle became a boomtown when gold was discovered in Alaska. Seattle was the departure point, and the miners' return to civilization. The following decade saw $200 million in gold come through Seattle from the north, the largest single shipment no less than one ton! Much of the profit was spent and invested in Seattle.

El Gaucho brings to mind this bygone era of elegance that was part of Seattle's growth. The spacious dining, the mink-lined booths, strolling Argentine guitarists, authentic charcoal broilers, and an extensive wine selection add up to an exquisite and expensive meal. In the words of Jack Kestenbaum, our audio man who introduced the restaurant to us, "you get what you pay for."

Canlis Restaurant is another place for a special evening. Cooking with dry vermouth was originated by Canlis during World War II, when wines were scarce. They say that in any recipe calling for white wine, dry vermouth can be used to improve bouquet and flavor. The "Canlis Shrimp" that follows calls for this. See what you think. There are also Canlis restaurants in San Francisco and Honolulu.

SEATTLE

Ivar's Acre of Clams is a great place to stop for a quick bite or "seafood to go" on the way to the Kingdome.

Photo by the author

VIKING SOUP

Ivar's

46 oz. fish stock
2 medium onions, diced
½ stalk celery, diced
12 oz. Half & Half
5 oz. halibut, cut in ½-in. cubes
5 oz. salmon, cut in ½-in. cubes
5 oz. shrimp meat
1 lb. potatoes, cooked
pinch parsley
1½ T. salt
1 T. MSG
1 tsp. white pepper
6 oz. butter
10 oz. flour

☐ Poach the fish in 6 cups of water. Use the water from the poached fish for stock. Add onions, celery, and cook until done. When done, add all other ingredients except butter and flour. Cook for 15 minutes. Mix flour and butter and add to soup. Stir over moderate heat for 10 minutes until it has thickened. Serve nice and hot with a tangy cole slaw and sour dough rolls. Serves 6.

POACHED FILET OF HALIBUT WITH DILL SAUCE

Ivar's

2 lb. Halibut filets, cut in 8-oz. portions
1 cup milk
4 oz. fresh dill
1 tsp. salt
¼ tsp. white pepper
pinch MSG
2 oz. flour
1 oz. butter
4 bay leaves

☐ Poach halibut in water with salt and bay leaves until fish flakes easily but is still moist, about 15 minutes.

Dill Sauce

☐ Put milk into saucepan with fresh dill, salt, pepper and MSG. Bring to boil and cook for 4 minutes.
Strain out fresh dill. Mix butter gradually with flour and stir until smooth. Slowly add to dill stock, cooking for 5 minutes.
Pour over each portion of halibut. Sprinkle with minced parsley and serve with boiled potato and lemon wedge. Serves 4.

110

SALMON WELLINGTON

Elliot's Bay Fish & Oyster Co.

2 salmon filets
stuffing (same as Snapper Duxelle)
Hollandaise sauce (same as Snapper Duxelle)
3 tarragon leaves
3 oz. tarragon vinegar
3 cups all-purpose flour
1 cup cake flour
6½ sticks unsalted butter
1½ tsp. salt
1 cup iced water

☐ If possible, use tail end of salmon to make stuffing pocket easier. If unavailable, angle-cut salmon to make filet and cut thin so it cooks fast. Add Duxelle stuffing and bay shrimp.

Puff Pastry

Mix flour, butter, and salt together rapidly to make large flakes. Blend in water. Remove from bowl and push, pat, and roll out on lightly floured surface. Roll out ½ inch thick, and flour side up. Cut in squares large enough to wrap around salmon. Lay dough on top of filet and flip over. Fold four points together and flip over again into square baking pan so points are under fish and top is smooth. Bake at 450° F. for 8 minutes, or until pastry shells are browned. To check, pierce tops with fork.

Optional

In a small pan, reduce tarragon leaves and tarragon vinegar until almost pasty. This can be mixed with Hollandaise sauce (see Snapper Duxelle) and served on top of puff pastry. Serves 2.

BARBECUE SALMON

Tillicum Village

☐ The salmon should be "booked," split along the length of the belly with the head removed.

The salmon is pulled down the split in a cedar stake, as far down as possible.

The cross-sticks, which are also cedar, are slipped between the cedar stake and the salmon, alternating sides and leaving a space of 6 to 8 inches between sticks on the same side. The cross-sticks are broken to fit the width of the salmon for ease of turning while they cook. Nowadays, instead of using cedar bark, a wire is wrapped around the top of the stick below the tail.

The fish are placed around an open alder wood fire with the flesh side toward the fire. The tail should lean slightly in toward the fire. The usual cooking time is about one hour, 45–50 minutes on the flesh side (or until flesh is firm.) Then the salmon are turned around, with the skin side facing the fire for 10–15 minutes.

CANLIS SHRIMP

Canlis Restaurant

28 large prawns, shelled (except tail), split, and cleaned
¼ cup butter
¼ cup dry vermouth
3 T. olive oil
3 T. lemon juice
1 small clove garlic, crushed
¼ tsp. salt
¼ tsp. fresh ground black pepper

☐ Pour olive oil into large skillet. When simmering, add shrimp and cook until golden brown. Turn shrimp over, reduce heat, add butter, garlic, salt and pepper. When well blended, raise heat to hot, add dry vermouth and lemon juice, constantly stirring or shaking skillet for one minute. Serve as an appetizer or dinner entree. Makes 4 servings.

Note: Cooking with dry vermouth was originated by Canlis during World War II when wines were scarce. Use in any recipe that calls for white wine and notice the improvement in bouquet and flavor. Also, use a tablespoon of dry vermouth over your steak, chops, or fish after they have been cooked. It will make a little "au jus" right on your plate.

With lobster: After you have broiled your lobster face down, turn it over and add a tablespoon of dry vermouth into the shell and let steam for about five minutes.

There's a good view and taste of the Seattle waterfront from inside Elliot Bay Fish & Oyster Co.

The talents of versatile quarterback Jim Zorn have not been enough to spark the Seahawks to the playoffs.

CANLIS SPECIAL SALAD

Canlis Restaurant

Originated by Canlis Restaurant in Honolulu, we offer this with no apologies to Caesar:

Salad
2 heads romaine
2 tomatoes, peeled

Condiments
¼ cup green onion, chopped
½ cup Romano cheese, freshly grated
1 lb. bacon, rendered, finely chopped
1 cup croutons

Dressing
1 cup olive oil
¼ cup lemon juice
½ tsp. fresh ground pepper
¼ tsp. fresh mint, chopped
¼ tsp. oregano
1 egg, coddled

☐ Into a large wooden bowl, pour approximately 2 tablespoons of good imported olive oil, sprinkle with salt, and rub firmly with a large clove of garlic. (The oil will act as a lubricant and the salt as an abrasive.) Remove garlic and, in the bottom of the bowl, first place the tomatoes cut in eighths, add romaine, sliced in 1-inch strips. You may add other salad vegetables if you choose, but remember to put the heavy vegetables in first with romaine on top. Add condiments.

Dressing: Pour the lemon juice and seasonings into a bowl. Add coddled egg and whip vigorously. Then add olive oil, whipping constantly.

When ready to serve, pour dressing over salad. Add croutons last. Toss vigorously. Serves 4–6.

SCALLOPS DIABLO

Stuart's

1½ lb. fresh scallops (approx. 30–40)
½ lb. fresh petite mushrooms
2 oz. butter, clarified
4 oz. red onion, julienne
4 oz. sweet red peppers, julienne
2 cloves garlic, minced
1 sprig parsley, minced
4 tsp. Dijon mustard
12 oz. heavy cream
4 oz. dry white wine
2 wedges fresh lemon
8 pats butter
salt and pepper, to taste

☐ This dish should be quickly sautéed or stir fried; adjust the timing of individual ingredients so that the vegetables remain crisp and the scallops do not become tough.

Sauté mushrooms in 2 oz. clarified butter; add onions and peppers and sauté another 2 minutes. Add scallops and cook half way through. Add minced garlic, parsley, squeeze of lemon, and white wine; reduce slightly and add cream.

When scallops are just short of being done remove them and vegetables from the pan. Continue to reduce the pan juices and cream to one half of its volume; stir in the Dijon mustard, remove from heat and swirl in the butter pats. Return the scallops and vegetables to the pan and coat with the sauce. Divide into four individual ramekins and serve.

RED SNAPPER DUXELLE

Elliot's Bay Fish & Oyster Co.

2 red snappers (boned and fileted)
4 oz. Alaskan bay shrimp
2 tsp. ham base (boullion)
2 strips bacon
1 onion
1 celery stalk
3 oz. white wine
4 eggs
4 oz. clarified butter
1 sprig fresh dill weed
salt, white pepper, Worcestershire sauce, and Tabasco sauce to taste
1 lemon
6 mushrooms

☐ "Butterfly" snapper (cut open lengthwise) to thin filet and make pocket for stuffing. Chop up bacon, onion, and celery, and brown in bacon grease. Add mushrooms (sliced) along with ham base and sauté. Let cool. Scoop 3 oz. of stuffing into pocket of each filet, or between the two halves if pocket splits; along

with 2 oz. of bay shrimp for each. Season to taste with salt, white pepper, Worcestershire sauce, Tabasco sauce, and fresh lemon. Bake at 450° F. for 6 minutes. Top with Hollandaise sauce. Serves 2.

Hollandaise Sauce

Blend egg yolks with clarified butter over low heat until smooth. Add wine, a squeeze of lemon, and dill weed.

QUILCENE OYSTERS IN BUTTER & WINE SAUCE

Ivar's

1 lb. oysters, drained
1 cup butter
½ cup sauterne
salt and pepper, to taste

☐ Melt butter gently in saucepan, add wine and simmer 2–3 minutes. Then add oysters. Simmer 3 minutes, being careful not to overcook oysters. Oysters should be hot all the way through. When oysters are heated, add salt and pepper to taste.

Serve oysters in sauce. Serves 4.

Photo by the author

113

TAMPA

On the first Monday following the first Tuesday each February, the fully rigged "José Gaspar" sails into Tampa Bay, manned with bloodthirsty buccaneers. After "pillaging" the town, they join in a parade of floats that wind their way through the downtown area, similar to Mardi Gras in New Orleans. The celebration commemorates an actual pillaging of Tampa by a band of pirates led by José Gasparilla. Such was the impact of the raid that the "Gasparilla Festival" is an annual event, and Tampa's football team is named the Buccaneers.

Ybor City, Tampa's Latin Quarter, has a colorful history as well. It was from here that José Marti, one of the leaders of the Cuban Revolution, led a successful campaign to free Cuba from Spanish rule. The world's largest Spanish restaurant, *Columbia,* has been here since 1905. Inside you'll find eleven dining rooms, strolling violinists and singers, jazz bands in the cafe and warehouse, and delicious food. *Fortune* magazine says it's Tampa's finest restaurant.

Some think *Bern's Steakhouse* is the best.

Specialties include aged prime beef and the world's largest wine list. Their wine list is larger than the Tampa-St. Petersburg phone book! The menu is as thorough as the wine list. It has a chart of the different cuts of beef, and the various thicknesses you may wish to have your beef carved (along with how well done you would like it, to bring out the best in the meat). They take great care in the preparation of the beef. Reservations at Bern's are strongly recommended. Bern Laxer, the owner, sent us a delicious idea for dessert, "Brazilian Snow," a fine way to end a meal.

The Kapok Tree Inn is in Clearwater, not far from Tampa. We thought it deserved a mention for its unique atmosphere. A large kapok tree grows in the center of a cocktail lounge decorated like a tropical garden. This is another very large restaurant, but the service is good, and prices are very reasonable. They feature steaks, seafood and chops. Corn fritters, or "hush puppies," are a local favorite served family-style, and your family will love them, too.

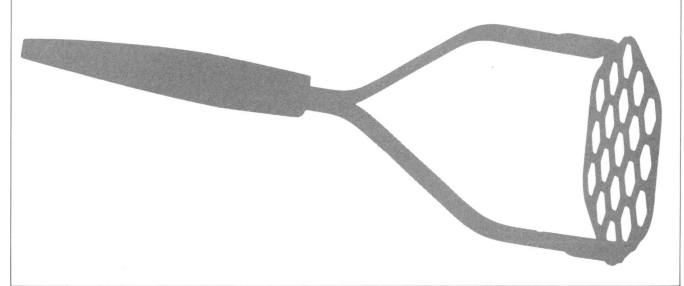

Garo Yepremian, a 15-year veteran of the NFL, is relatively new but successful at kicking for the Bucs.

SPANISH BEAN SOUP

Columbia Restaurant

¼ lb. garbanzos
1 lb. potatoes, quartered
4 oz. salt pork
2 chorizos (Spanish sausage)
8 oz. ham, cut in chunks
1 onion, chopped
2 qt. water
1 T. salt

☐ After washing beans thoroughly, soak them over-night with a tablespoon of salt and sufficient water to more than cover the beans. Morning after, drain salted water from beans. Add two quarts of water and ham. Simmer 45 minutes. In the meantime, fry salt pork, adding chopped onions. Do not brown, fry until transparent. Add this and potatoes to beans and salt (if needed) and cook until potatoes are done. Remove from fire and add chorizos cut in thin slices. Serves 4.

BRAZILIAN SNOW

Bern's Steak House

1 pt. best quality vanilla ice cream, softened slightly
4–6 round T. fresh coffee, roasted but unground
whipped cream

☐ To prepare this simple dessert, you will need a small nut grinder that can be found in a department store or health food store.

Grind the coffee as finely as you can. Then sprinkle about one-third of it over the ice cream. Now scoop up the ice cream, one scoopful at a time. Try to mix the two together without overhandling the ice cream.

As you finish one layer of ice cream, sprinkle more coffee over the top, and continue until all of the coffee and all of the ice cream is in serving dishes.

Then top with whipped cream and sprinkle the last of the pulverized coffee over the whipped cream. Garnish with a cherry and serve at once. Serves 4.

Remember that coffee loses its flavor soon after it's ground and shouldn't be used again after 5 or 10 minutes if you want the maximum fresh coffee taste.

CORN FRITTERS

Kapok Tree Inn

1 cup flour, sifted
1½ tsp. baking powder
1 T. sugar
1 scant tsp. salt
1 egg
¼ cup milk
½ cup whole kernel corn, canned
deep fat, for frying

☐ Resift flour, baking powder, sugar, and salt together. Add egg, milk, and corn and stir until well blended. Heat deep fat to 350° F. and then drop batter into fat by the teaspoonful. Fry until golden brown, turning once to cook evenly. Drain fritter on paper towel. Place on serving platter and sprinkle with confectioner's sugar.

Makes about 16 fritters.

SPANISH CUSTARD (FLAN)

Columbia

3 cups sugar
6 eggs
1 tsp. vanilla
1 tsp. ground anisette
pinch salt
1 pt. boiling milk

☐ Boil a cup of sugar and half a cup of water until brown, then pour the caramel into six molds. Beat eggs, add two cups of sugar, vanilla, ground anisette, pinch of salt and beat again. Add pint of boiling milk little by little, then strain through cloth or china colander.

Pour mixture into molds, put molds in water-filled pan and bake for 30 minutes at 350° F. in oven. Don't let water boil, or custard will be filled with holes. Cool in refrigerator. When ready to serve, press edges of custard with spoon to break away from mold, then turn upside down. The caramel then tops the custard. Serves 6.

PAELLA VALENCIANA

Columbia

½ lb. pork, cut in chunks
½ fryer, quartered
1 lb. lobster, in chunks
½ lb. shrimp, peeled
8 oysters, shucked
8 scallops
8 mussels
4 clams, in shells
4 stone crab claws
1 lb. red snapper, in chunks
6 cups fresh seafood or chicken stock, or bottled
    clam juice
small green peas, asparagus, and sliced pimientos
    for garnish
1 onion, chopped
1 green pepper, chopped
3 cloves garlic, minced
1 bay leaf
½ cup whole tomatoes
½ cup olive oil
1½ cups rice
1 tsp. salt
pinch saffron
¼ cup white wine

☐ Pour oil in heavy casserole. Add onion and green pepper; fry until limp, but not brown. Chop tomatoes in blender. Add with garlic and bay leaf. Cook for 5 minutes. Add pork and chicken, and sauté until tender, stirring to prevent sticking or burning.

Add seafood and stock. When this boils, add rice and saffron. Stir. Let it come to a boil, cover and bake in oven at 350° F. for 20 minutes. When ready to serve,

sprinkle with wine and garnish with peas, asparagus, and pimiento.

This extremely versatile dish allows you to use almost any native seafood in lieu of the stated ingredients. It is the national dish of Spain. Serves 4.

RED SNAPPER "ALICANTE"

Columbia

2 lb. red snapper
2 Spanish onions
¾ cup brown beef stock gravy
½ cup Spanish olive oil
1 tsp. salt
4 green peppers
4 cloves fresh garlic
pinch pepper
1 cup white Spanish wine
¼ cup almonds, sliced and toasted
8 shrimp supreme
8 pieces eggplant, breaded and fried
parsley

☐ Place the snapper on top of slices of onions; spread over the bottom of casserole.

Over the fish, pour olive oil, salt, pepper, brown gravy, and the white wine. Also add green pepper rings.

Bake at 350° F. for approximately 25 minutes.

Garnish with breaded eggplant rings, shrimp supreme, sliced almonds, and parsley. Serves 4.

CHICKEN AND YELLOW RICE

Columbia

1 2½-lb. fryer, quartered
1 large onion, chopped
3 cloves garlic, minced
1 large green pepper, chopped
½ cup whole tomatoes (chop or whirl in blender)
1 bay leaf
2 cups chicken broth or water
2 cups rice
2 tsp. salt
pinch saffron
⅓ cup olive oil
¼ cup white wine

☐ Pour olive oil in a heavy casserole or clay pot. Add onions and green pepper, cook over medium heat until tender but not brown. Add garlic and tomatoes, cook for 5 minutes. Add chicken and sauté vegetables and chicken. Add liquid and saffron. Cook until chicken is almost tender. Now add rice, stir well. When it starts to boil again, cover casserole and bake in 350° F. oven for 20 minutes.

When ready to serve, sprinkle with wine and garnish with small green peas and strips of pimientos. Serves 4.

WASHINGTON, D.C.

In 1791, President George Washington chose the site and the man he wanted to plan the new U.S. capital. A year later, Parisian-born designer Pièrre l'Enfant completed his design. There is a similarity to the layout of the expanse of Versailles in France, and the broad avenues and sweeping vistas of the capital. Combined with the monumental buildings and the riches they contain, Washington, D.C. is unique among American cities.

Michael Lautier of *Rive Gauche* has brought the French influence to the capital as well. For a fine evening, we strongly recommend his place. If you can't get to Washington, D.C., then try their "Côte de Veau Sauté aux Morelles." It translates to veal chops sautéed with mushrooms, but it sounds so much better in French.

El Tio Pepe is a Spanish restaurant on M Street in Old Georgetown. The paella is what brings us there, so "Paella" is what Mr. Cesa, the owner, sent. This recipe can be used for either fish or meat.

If seafood is your favorite we think you'll like *John Mandis Market Inn*. It claims 101 varieties of seafood, including live lobsters, fresh daily. They are open seven nights a week, serving dinner until 1 a.m., except on Sunday when the kitchen closes at midnight. They have live music and a nice atmosphere. John Curran, our friend there, sent along a rich and creamy recipe for "She-Crab Soup." A capital idea.

A restaurant where you're likely to see some of the capital's well-known figures is *The Palm*. Sister restaurant to the ones mentioned in New York, it serves the same great steaks and seafood.

One of the greatest rivalries in pro football is between the Baltimore Colts and the Washington Redskins. We were fortunate to have one of these thrillers on a Monday Night game in 1979. The reason for the rivalry is the proximity of these two major cities to one another. They even share the same international airport: Baltimore–Washington International. We discovered a very nice restaurant in the airport during a layover. *C.K.'s,* named after a legendary World War I flying ace, has excellent service, pleasant atmosphere, well-prepared food, and the "small touches," (like the slice of lemon in the drinking water) that can make you feel good even when travelling has got you down.

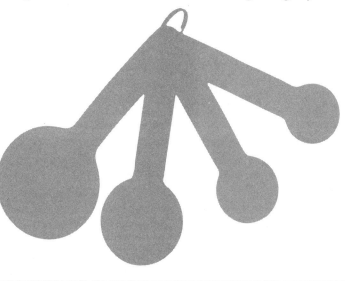

Photo by Jim Conroy

CÔTE DE VEAU SAUTÉ AUX MORELLES
(Veal Chops Sautéed with Mushrooms)

Rive Gauche

4 8-oz. veal chops
2 oz. morelles; if not available, use sliced white
    mushrooms
8 oz. heavy cream
4 oz. brown stock
2 oz. Madeira
2 oz. butter
2 tsp. shallots, chopped
salt and pepper

☐ Season the chops with salt, pepper, and flour. Cook them slowly in a sauté pan with butter; then place the chops on the service tray. Throw out the cooking grease and add the shallots and mushrooms. Sauté them for a few seconds then add the Madeira and allow it to cook for 5 minutes. Taste for seasoning, then pour the sauce over the chops and serve. Serves 4.

PAELLA

El Tio Pepe

Rice: approximately ¼ cup per serving
Meat and/or shellfish: ½ cup or more per serving of
    the following: chicken, rabbit, beef and/or shell-
    fish
Vegetables: 1 large ripe tomato; peas; pimientos and
    fresh lemon wedges for garnish
Liquid: A good stock made out of chicken bones,
    celery, leeks, tomatoes, carrots, etc. (Instant
    bouillon chicken flavor can serve as substitute.)

Approximately 2 measures liquid to 1 measure rice.
Seasonings: saffron, salt, black pepper to taste
Olive oil: Approximately 1½ ounces per serving

☐ Brown desired quantity of cubed meat and/or shellfish in preheated oil; add chopped tomato, ground black pepper, mixing well. Add desired quantity of green peas; continue cooking over high heat until well done. At this point, add the rice and brown slightly, mixing it well. Add the correct amount of water, a pinch or two of saffron, and cook over high heat until rice is about half done. Lower heat and simmer until water is absorbed. If more liquid is necessary, add only boiling liquid.

Allow paella to stand a few minutes before serving. Garnish with red pimientos and lemon wedges.

SHE-CRAB SOUP

John Mandis Market Inn

1 qt. Half & Half
4 T. flour
4 T. butter
3 T. paprika
⅓ 1-lb. can backfin crabmeat
¼ cup sherry
salt and pepper, to taste

☐ Under low flame, melt butter in saucepan and slowly add flour. Stir until golden brown. Add Half & Half, stirring slowly until sauce thickens. Add salt and pepper to taste. Add paprika and sherry. Add crabmeat and let stand one-half hour to allow soup to properly season. Top each serving with a ball of whipped cream.

HAWAII

HAWAII

Halftime, Hawaiian style.

One of the greatest benefits of covering professional football for ABC is our commitment to televise the Pro Bowl each year. What makes this such a pleasure is the fact that the game has been in Honolulu, Hawaii, the last few years. The Hawaiian football fans love it, the players love it, and we love it. We thought we'd add a special chapter for Hawaii in the hope the Pro Bowl game stays there forever. After all, it gives us a chance for a Hawaiian vacation each year!

On one visit, Jack Dorfman, the marketeer cameraman (the roving camera on wheels along the sideline) discovered the Coco Palms Resort on Kuaii, the island next to Oahu. He told the rest of us about this little bit of paradise. It is run by the Guslanders, a couple who know how to make people feel good on their vacation. An Elvis Presley classic, *Blue Hawaii*, was filmed here, and just down the road is the Opaekaa Falls, the cascading waterfall seen at the opening of *Fantasy Island* each week on ABC. From the *Coconut Palace Dining Room* come these tasty Hawaiian treats. Mahalo.

MACADAMIA NUT CHIFFON PIE

Coconut Palace Dining Room

3 egg yolks
¼ cup sugar
1 cup milk
1 envelope unflavored gelatin
¼ cup water
¼ cup macadamia nut bits
3 egg whites
½ tsp. cream of tartar
¼ cup sugar
1 baked pie shell (recipe below)
1 cup Avoset whipping cream
3 T. sugar
2 T. macadamia nut bits

☐ Soften gelatin in cold water. Hold for use later.
Combine yolks, ¼ cup sugar, and milk. Cook over medium heat until mixture has thickened. Remove from heat and blend in softened gelatin. Chill over iced water until mixture starts to gel. Whip egg whites and cream of tartar until stiff. Add ¼ cup sugar gradually.
Fold in chilled mixture and pour into a cold baked

pie shell. Chill until firm, top with whipped cream and macadamia nut bits.

Pie Crust

1 cup flour
¼ cup shortening
¼ cup butter
¼ tsp. salt

Cut shortening and butter into flour and salt until lumps are pea-sized. Add 2 tablespoons cold water and stir until mixture is moistened. Roll out in pan and prick crust. Bake at 400° F. for 15 minutes. Makes one 9-in. crust.

CHICKEN IN A COCONUT

Coconut Palace Dining Room

1 whole coconut with husk
¾ lb. chicken breast
¼ lb. fresh mushrooms
3 shallots, chopped
2 T. butter
2 T. flour
1 cup milk
½ cup coconut milk
¼ cup sherry
¼ tsp. curry powder
salt and pepper, to taste
2 cups mashed potatoes
2 T. coconut, shredded

☐ Saw coconut in half, with husk on. Melt butter, then add flour and cook for 2 minutes. Add milk to make cream sauce. Dice chicken breast and sauté with salt, pepper, and curry powder. Add mushrooms, shallots, and sherry. Simmer, then add cream sauce, and coconut milk.

Pipe border of mashed potatoes, fill chicken mixture in cavity of coconut. Sprinkle top with shredded coconut and bake until potatoes are brown.

GREEN PAPAYA SOUP

Coconut Palace Dining Room

5 green papaya
2 cups chicken broth
5 oz. chicken breast
½ tsp. fresh ginger
4 tsp. butter

☐ Simmer ginger in chicken broth for 15 minutes. Remove. Peel, seed and cut 1 papaya into thin 1 in. strips. Cut chicken breast into 1-in. strips. Sauté chicken breast and green papaya until soft. Add to broth. Cut 4 papayas one inch from stem end and scoop out seeds with a melon baller. Fill papaya cavity with chicken broth, sit upright in water and simmer until slightly tender in pot. Remove.

Pour chicken broth into hot papaya cup and replace papaya top (stem end) and serve. Serves 4.

Photo by ABC Sports

Why is Lynn Swann smiling? Announcers are out-of-bounds.

KUPA ULA
(Lobster Bisque)

Island Holidays

¼ cup oil
1 carrot, chopped
½ onion, sliced
½ tsp. thyme
1 bay leaf
1 tomato, chopped
2 lb. raw lobster
2 T. cognac, warmed
¼ cup white wine
3 cups fish stock
¾ rice, raw
salt, pepper, Tabasco, to taste
½ cup heavy cream

☐ Heat oil in pot. Add vegetables, herbs, and lobster and cook until lobster skin turns red. Add cognac and flame it; then add white wine. Simmer 5 minutes.

Remove lobster and keep warm. Add fish stock, rice, salt, pepper. Simmer 45 minutes.

Press through a sieve or whirl in a blender. Return to stove and add cream. Correct seasoning. Add pieces of lobster meat and serve. Serves 6.

PART II

Photo by ABC Sports

THE ABC CREW'S FAVORITE RECIPES

It takes some sixty people to bring Monday Night Football to the screen each week. Among these people are the announcers, production crew, and engineering crew that make everything work. Although we come from different backgrounds, and have different skills, once a week we bring it all together to put the game on the air. One thing we all have in common is that we miss our loved ones at home while we are away. Here are a few recipes from some of the crew members and their spouses. No matter how great a restaurant dinner may be, there's no place like home.

THE CREW

Donatelli and cameraman Tom O'Connell take a halftime break.

Photo by Nancy O'Connell

MOM'S APPLE PIE

Audrey Donatelli

Seems like everyone we shoot says "Hi, Mom"; so we thought this could be our chance. After all, what would a cookbook of American cuisine be without "Mom's Apple Pie"? This recipe is from Mrs. Audrey Donatelli of Tucker, Ga. Thanks, Mom.

5–7 tart apples
¾–1 cup sugar
2 T. flour
⅛ tsp. salt
1 tsp. cinnamon
¼ tsp. nutmeg
1 recipe plain pastry
2 T. butter

☐ Pare apples and slice thin; add sugar mixed with flour, salt, and spices; fill 9-inch deep dish pastry-lined pie pan. Dot with butter. Adjust to crust. Bake in hot oven (450° F.) 10 minutes. If apples aren't tart, add 1 tablespoon lemon juice. Grated lemon rind may also be added, if desired.

Plain Pastry

2½ cups flour
1 tsp. salt
¾ cup shortening
5–6 T. cold water or milk

Sift flour and salt; cut in shortening with two knives or pastry blender until size of crumbs resembles small peas. Add water, a tablespoon at a time, mixing and pressing ingredients together with fork. Turn out onto waxed paper; press pastry firmly together. Form in 2 balls. Chilling dough facilitates handling. Milk may be used in place of water for a slightly browner crust of very nice flavor.

VEAL TOMMY O'

Nancy and Tom O'Connell

This is a recipe that Tom (cameraman) liked so much, he got the chef at Portofino's Restaurant in Cleveland (now closed) to jot it down. The name has been changed from Veal Portofino to Veal Tommy O'.

2 or 3 veal cutlets
½ lb. butter
½ cup flour
1 clove garlic, finely chopped
scallions, finely chopped, including green stalk
mushrooms, sliced
cooking sherry, to taste

☐ Dust the veal with the flour. Sauté in frying pan with about half a stick of butter. Pour off the butter, and add the rest of the butter along with the scallions, mushrooms, and garlic. Add the cooking sherry to taste, and sauté at a low heat. Serve with linguine as a side dish. Serves 1–2.

PAPPY'S POPOVERS

Joan Ciampi

Joan, a production assistant, sends us something to start the day with and something to end it: popovers and strawberry zabaglione.

1 cup all-purpose flour
1 tsp. salt
3 eggs
1 cup milk
2 T. whipping cream

☐ Stir flour and salt together. Make well in center; add eggs, milk, and cream. Beat for 3 minutes. Cover batter; chill thoroughly for 2 hours. Heat muffin pan thoroughly in a very hot oven. (450° F) Grease quickly with oil. Fill cups almost to brim; return to oven. Bake for 22 minutes; reduce temperature to 375° F., bake 13 minutes longer.

Loosen popovers from pan, and serve immediately. Serves 8.

126

STRAWBERRY ZABAGLIONE

Joan Ciampi

2 large egg yolks
⅓ cup sweet Marsala
3 T. sugar
1 cup heavy cream
1 T. confectioner's sugar
½ tsp. vanilla
3 cups strawberries, hulled and halved

☐   In top of double boiler, set over simmering water. Combine egg yolks, sweet Marsala, and 3 table-spoons sugar. With an electric mixer, beat the mixture at high speed for 5 minutes, or until it is fluffy and almost tripled in volume. Transfer mixture to bowl; set in ice, stir until cold.

In chilled bowl beat heavy cream, confectioner's sugar, and vanilla until it holds stiff peaks; fold into mixture.

Divide strawberries among 6 champagne glasses, spoon zabaglione over them. Serves 6.

CREAM CHEESE "CAPCAKES"

Em and Tony Capitano

Tony "Cap" is a video operator—one of the guys who tune cameras so the picture looks great on your home TV. He's so proud of his wife's cooking that we've called Em's recipe "Capcakes."

16 oz. cream cheese
1½ cups sugar
1 tsp. vanilla extract
4 eggs
graham cracker crumbs
canned cherries, blueberries, etc.

☐   Preheat oven 350° F. Line a large cupcake tin (for 12 muffins) with cupcake liners. Sprinkle with graham cracker crumbs.

Blend cream cheese, eggs, vanilla, sugar to-gether. Fill tins three-quarters full and bake for 20 minutes. Turn oven off but keep oven door closed. Keep cupcakes in oven until it cools. Refrigerate. Top with fruit.

PEANUT-CHOCOLATE DESSERT

Joyce and Jack Kestenbaum

Jack, our audio man better known as "The Mus-tache", has been raving about this dessert for months. It is delicious. With that cookie duster of his we won-der if any of the shaved chocolate ever makes it to his mouth!

½ cup butter, softened
1 cup all-purpose flour
⅔ cup peanuts, finely chopped, dry roasted
1 8-oz. package cream cheese, softened

Photo by ABC Sports

Audio man Jack Kestenbaum, also known as "The Moustache," may put the Reese's people out of business with his favorite dessert.

⅓ cup peanut butter
1 cup confectioner's sugar
1 12-oz. carton frozen whipped topping, thawed and divided
1 4½-oz. package vanilla instant pudding and pie filling mix
2¾ cups milk
1 1.2-oz. bar milk chocolate, shaved
⅓ cup peanuts, chopped, dry roasted

☐   Cut butter into flour until mixture resembles coarse meal; stir ⅔ cup peanuts into flour mixture. Press pea-nut mixture into a 13 x 9 x 2-in. baking pan. Bake at 350° F. for 20 minutes; cool completely. Combine cream cheese, peanut butter, and confectioner's sugar; beat until fluffy. Stir 1 cup whipped topping into cream cheese mixture. Spread over crust. Chill.

Combine pudding mix and milk; beat 2 minutes at medium speed of electric mixer. Spread pudding over cream cheese layer. Spread remaining whipped topping over pudding layer. Sprinkle the top with shaved chocolate and ⅓ cup chopped peanuts. Store in refrigerator.

127

THE CREW

Andy Armentani.

Photo by Nancy O'Connell

MUSSELS WITH EGGS

From the House of Fontana, Cresskill, N.J.

Andy Armentani, a bachelor who enjoys good food, knows a thing or two about cooking. These are a few of his favorite dishes. The Fontanas of Cresskill, N.J., are some of his favorite people. As relatives you could call his "foster family," they've prepared a number of monumental meals over the years with "Uncle Andy" as the guest of honor. When asked how it was, Andy answers in his best Italian (his eyes roll, his hands gesture, and his mouth goes "Ahhh . . ."). The printing of their recipes along with his is a way of sharing his favorites with us, and thanking the Fontanas for making their place "home."

3 lbs. mussels
5 eggs
5 cloves of garlic, chopped
3 Tbsp. of dry parsley
½ cup of grated Romano cheese
2 Tbsp. of olive oil

☐ Scrape and clean mussels. In a large pot, steam mussels until they open fully. Place steamed mussels on the half shell in a 15-in. by 2-in. oblong pan. Strain and reserve mussel juice. In a large bowl combine eggs, garlic, parsley, cheese, oil, and mussel juice. Mix well. Pour this mixture over mussels and sprinkle bread crumbs on top. Bake at 350° F. until egg mixture is firm and golden.

PASTA AND PEAS
(Pasta Con Piselli)

4 quarts of water
1 teaspoon of salt
1 lb. small or medium-size shell, elbow, or ditalini macaroni
¼ cup of olive oil
½ cup of chopped onion
1 cup of tomatoes, sieved
¾ teaspoon of salt
¼ teaspoon of black pepper
⅛ teaspoon of oregano
4 cups (1 can) of peas
Grated parmesan or Romano cheese

☐ Bring to a boil the 4 quarts of water with 1 teaspoon of salt in a large saucepan. Slowly add the pasta, boil rapidly, uncovered, 10 to 12 minutes or until pasta is cooked. Reserve 3 cups of water, and drain pasta into a colander or sieve. Set aside. Heat in a large saucepan the olive oil; add the chopped onions and cook until transparent, cook the onions slowly, then add the mixture of tomatoes, salt, pepper, and oregano slowly. Simmer about 10 minutes and add the cooked pasta, reserved water and peas. Simmer about 10 minutes. Serve and top with grated cheese. Serves 4 to 6.

LINGUINI WITH WHITE CLAM SAUCE
(Pasta con Salsa Alle Vongole)

Joan Fontana

1 pound of linguini
¼ cup olive oil
2 cloves garlic, chopped
¼ cup clam juice
1 tsp. chopped parsley
1 tsp. salt
½ teaspoon oregano
½ teaspoon black pepper
⅛ teaspoon crushed red hot pepper
9 to 12 clams cut into pieces (save juice)

☐ Heat olive oil in a skillet and lightly brown garlic. Slowly stir in ¼ cup of clam juice; stir in parsley, salt, pepper, oregano. Then slowly add clams with ¼ to ½ cup of clam juice. Cook until clams are heated—approximately 3 to 5 minutes. Pour over the cooked linguini. This recipe can be made with shell macaroni instead of linguini if so desired.

128

PASTA CON FAGIOLI
(Macaroni and Bean Soup)

A. J. Armentani

2 cups of either ditalini, small shells, or elbow macaroni
2 Tbsp. olive oil
2 cloves garlic, finely chopped
1½ Tbsp. parsley, finely chopped
½ teaspoon salt
¼ teaspoon black pepper
⅛ lb. Prosciutto
2 cups cooked white beans (1 can with liquid)
1 cup tomatoes, sieved
1 quart of warm water
Grated Parmesan cheese
Crushed hot pepper (optional)

☐ Heat olive oil in large saucepan, add garlic and brown. Add parsley, tomatoes, salt, and black pepper; cook and stir for 10 minutes. Add warm water and beans and bring to a boil. Cook about 10 minutes. Stir in the pasta and boil uncovered for 10 to 12 minutes or until the macaroni is cooked; stir frequently to keep from sticking. Serve hot and top with grated cheese. Add crushed red hot pepper if so desired. Makes 4 to 6 generous portions.

STUFFED CALAMARI
(Squid)

Joan Fontana

6 medium size squid, cleaned
3 eggs
2 large cloves of garlic, finely chopped
2 Tbsp. of fresh parsley, finely chopped
2 Tbsp. of olive oil
Romano cheese
Bread crumbs

☐ Pre-heat oven to 400° F. Wash squid thoroughly and drain well. Combine eggs, garlic, parsley, and oil in a large bowl; mix well. Then add equal amounts of grated cheese and bread crumbs until it gets like a stuffing mix (not too dry). Stuff bodies of squid halfway with mixture and fasten opening with a wooden toothpick. Arrange squid in a deep baking pan.

Sauce

1 large can of plum tomatoes, chopped
2 cloves of garlic, chopped
2 Tbsp. of parsley, chopped
¼ cup of olive oli
Salt and pepper to taste

☐ Combine all ingredients in a large bowl and mix well. Pour over squid and sprinkle Romano cheese on top. Bake in a 400° F. oven for 15 minutes, then turn over to 350° F for about 50 minutes or until squid are tender.

This also makes an excellent sauce to pour over a bed of linguini.

CHICKEN CACCIATORE

A. J. Armentani

½ cup olive oil
3 cloves garlic, cut
1 frying chicken, 2 to 3 pounds ready-to-cook weight
½ cup white flour
1½ teaspoons salt
¼ teaspoon black pepper
2 eggs
¼ cup milk
1 Tbsp. chopped parsley
1 medium onion, sliced thin
½ lb. mushrooms
2 green peppers, cut into ½-inch strips
4 cups tomatoes, sieved
1 teaspoon salt
½ teaspoon black pepper
1 teaspoon oregano or Italian seasoning
½ cup of white wine

☐ Disjoint and cut chicken into serving pieces. Rinse and pat dry. To coat chicken evenly, shake two or three pieces at a time in a plastic bag containing the mixture of salt, flour, and black pepper. Combine the 2 eggs, well beaten, with milk and parsley. Heat olive oil and garlic until brown in a heavy skillet. Dip each piece of chicken in egg mixture, starting with meaty pieces, and place them in skillet skin-side down; add less meaty pieces as others brown. Brown all sides by turning with tongs or two spoons. While chicken is browning, combine tomatoes, salt, pepper, oregano and add to browned chicken slowly. Cook onions, peppers, and mushrooms in 3 tablespoons of butter or margarine until mushrooms are lightly browned and onions are transparent. Add to chicken with tomato mixture and add parsley. Cook slowly 25 or 30 minutes or until thickest pieces of chicken are tender. Add white wine 2 minutes before end.

ZITI AND BROCCOLI

A. J. Armentani

☐ In a large saucepan, bring 4 quarts of water to a boil. Add 2 teaspoons of salt, and gradually add 1 pound of ziti. Boil rapidly, uncovered, 10 to 12 minutes or until ziti is cooked firm. Reserve 3 cups of liquid. Drain ziti into a colander and set aside.

Cook 1 pound of broccoli until just tender, set aside. In a large sauce pan, heat ¼ cup of olive oil and 2 cloves of garlic, chopped; add drained broccoli and ziti with the 3 cups of reserved liquid. Season with ¼ teaspoon of pepper and simmer 10 minutes. Serve topped with grated Parmesan or Romano cheese. Some people may wish to add hot crushed red pepper. Serves 4 to 6 people.

THE CREW

Dandy Don and the Giffer have given up playing football, but they haven't forgotten the best football cities to play in.

CARPACCIO

Susan and Don Meredith

Don and Susan have helped considerably on our project. Here are a few recipes from some of their favorite restaurants around the country: "Carpaccio" from La Scala, "Lobster Cioppini" from Conti's Cross Keys Inn, and "Filet Stephanie" from Le Chateaubriand Le Pavillon Hotel. They also sent a favorite recipe for "Pimiento Cheese Ball."

1 T. Worcestershire sauce
1 cup mayonnaise (preferably homemade)
½ tsp. Tabasco sauce
½ tsp. dry mustard
⅓ cup strong beef stock
1 lb. filet mignon, very lean

☐ Mix first four ingredients until well-blended. Mixture should be very thick.

Slowly beat in approximately ⅓ cup of strong beef stock. Chill.

Put filet mignon into freezer. After 20 minutes, remove meat and slice paper thin with electric knife. Arrange in circle on individual plates.

In a decorative manner, pour sauce partially over meat. Garnish with capers and cornichons. Serves 6.

LOBSTER CIOPPINI

Susan and Don Meredith

1¼ lb. lobster
¼ cup olive oil
1 clove garlic, chopped
2 large ripe tomatoes, chopped
1 tsp. parsley, chopped
1 tsp. basil, chopped
½ tsp. dry oregano
1 cup clam broth
1 pinch cayenne
1 pinch fennel seeds
1 T. butter
6 little neck clams
8–10 mussels, cleaned
3 large shrimp, de-shelled and split
¼ cup white wine
1 cup wide noodles, cooked
4 slices garlic toast rounds

☐ Steam lobster. Remove cavity. Set aside and keep warm.

In large, deep (preferably iron) stewing kettle, add oil and chopped garlic till transparent. Add tomatoes, parsley, basil, dry oregano, and cook until hot. Add clam broth, butter, whole clams, and mussels. Cook until shells are open.

Add white wine and cayenne. Place lobster and raw shrimp in kettle (liquid should nearly cover all items). Add fennel.

In deep-dish platter, place cooked noodles. Add cioppini on top. Arrange garlic rounds on top and sides. Garnish with sprig of parsley. Serves 1.

PIMIENTO CHEESE BALL
Susan and Don Meredith

¼ cup green pepper, minced
¼ cup onion, minced
½ cup pimiento, chopped
⅓ cup mayonnaise
1 cup whipped cream cheese, room temperature
2 T. sherry
1 T. seeded jalapenos, chopped
1 large package Velveeta, room temperature
½ cup mild cheddar cheese, room temperature
dash Worcestershire sauce

☐ Mix all ingredients well. Serve at room temperature with Fritos, crackers, or crudités!

FILET STEPHANIE
Susan and Don Meredith

2 oz. ground veal
1 tsp. parsley, chopped
½ tsp. garlic, chopped
½ tsp. shallots, chopped
1 egg
1 T. bread crumbs
½ tsp. mint leaves, chopped
½ oz. Madeira wine
salt and pepper, to taste
1 4-oz. filet mignon
1 T. butter
puff pastry

☐ In bowl, mix all ingredients well, except filet mignon, butter, and puff pastry. Set aside. Preheat oven to 425° F.

In skillet, melt butter until hot.

Add filet mignon and sauté 40 seconds each side. Remove.

Arrange cooked filet in center of baking dish. Surround with veal mixture. Circle this with a 2 x 6-in. strip of puff pastry.

Brush 1 beaten egg on pastry dough.

In 425° F. oven, bake until pastry is golden brown. Remove and place on dinner plate. Pour 1 cup béarnaise sauce over filet. Serves 1.

WIENER SCHNITZEL
Astrid and Frank Gifford

Astrid makes some great German food. Here's a meal featuring Weiner Schnitzel. She emphasizes using French bread crumbs if possible. They really add something.

6 veal scallops, pounded very thin
2 eggs, beaten with a little water
flour
butter, clarified
2 cups French bread crumbs
butter, lemon, and chopped fresh parsley

☐ Dip scallops first in flour, then egg/water mixture, and finally in bread crumbs. Melt clarified butter (or mixture of ½ butter and ½ oil) in pan, and cook scallops *hot* just 2 minutes a side—until golden brown. Melt juice of lemon, butter, and parsley and pour over scallops before serving.

HEARTY CHEESE AND VEGETABLE SOUP
Astrid and Frank Gifford

2 cups celery, chopped
2 cups carrots, chopped
1 cup leeks, chopped
2 cups broccoli
2 cups Havarti cheese, grated
½ cup Jarlsberg cheese
1 pt. heavy cream
salt and pepper to taste
¼–½ tsp. cayenne pepper
1 13¾-oz. can chicken broth

☐ Bring broth to boil. Boil all vegetables just 3 minutes in broth. Add cheese and cook until melted. Add cream. Thicken with flour/butter paste or cornstarch/water. Add salt, pepper, and cayenne. Serves 8.

PURÉED ZUCCHINI SOUP
Astrid and Frank Gifford

2 large zucchini
2 13¾ oz. cans chicken broth
2 medium onions, peeled and sectioned
2 medium potatoes
3 T. sour cream
salt and pepper

☐ Chop zucchini coarsely. Boil in chicken broth with onions and potatoes 30 minutes. Drain, retaining a few tablespoons of liquid and put in blender with salt, pepper, and 3 tablespoons sour cream. Serve hot or cold with dollop of sour cream on top. Serves 6.

Tape operator Martin Bell and cameraman Steve Wolff figure the tee-shirts help when they forget what they're doing.

REVERSE ANGLE CHILI

Stephanie and Steve Wolff

Steve's got a lonely job. When you're the "reverse angle" cameraman, you're always on the other side of the field. Some nights the wind blows and it's chilly. So the Wolffs offer "Reverse Angle Chili" and "Charcoal-Broiled Potatoes" to warm you on a cold night.

1¼ lb. hot Italian sausage, cut in 1-in. pieces
1¼ lb. ground steak or swiss steak, cut in ½-in. cubes
6–8 pieces of bacon, cut in 1-in. pieces
½ lb. fresh mushrooms, sliced
2–3 onions, chopped
1 green pepper, seeded and chopped
3 jalapeno peppers, finely chopped
3 hot red peppers, crushed
3 cloves garlic, crushed
2–4 T. chili powder
1 T. Worcestershire sauce
½ tsp. dry mustard
1 large can tomatoes
1 32-oz. can kidney beans, drained
½ cup (approx.) red wine
fresh ground pepper and salt to taste.

☐ Brown bacon, drain and pat dry. Brown steak. Brown and cook sausage well; drain. Place meat in range pot. Sauté mushrooms, onions, and green peppers. Combine with meat.

Add chopped tomatoes and juice to meat along with kidney beans. Add remaining ingredients. Bring to boil and reduce to low heat. Simmer uncovered for 3–4 hours, adding water if needed. Serve in bowl with sour cream and grated cheese on top. Serves 6.

CHARCOAL-BROILED POTATOES

Stephanie and Steve Wolff

4 baking potatoes
4 T. butter
season with salt and pepper

☐ Wash potatoes and leave skin on. Cut in ¼-in. lengthwise pieces. Melt butter in pan. Dip potatoes in melted butter. Season to taste. Place potatoes face down on warm coals and season other side. Keep cooking about 20 minutes or until cooked inside.

OATMEAL CHOCOLATE CHIP BARS

Jeanne and Lou Rende

Lou shows the instant replays, and after tasting one of Jeanne's recipes, you'll demand a replay.

¼ cup margarine or butter
½ cup brown sugar
3 T. water
1 cup oatmeal
½ cup flour
½ tsp. baking powder
¼ tsp. salt
1½ tsp. vanilla
1 cup chocolate chips

☐ Cream butter and brown sugar. Sift together flour, baking powder, and salt. Add alternately with vanilla and water. Fold in oatmeal and chocolate chips. Place in greased 8-in. square pan. Bake in 375° F. oven for 25 minutes. Cool, but cut bars while still slightly warm.
Note: To double recipe, use one 9 x 13-in. pan.

SALMON CHEESE BALL

Jeanne and Lou Rende

1 1-lb. can (2 cups) salmon
1 8-oz. package cream cheese, softened
1 T. lemon juice
1 small onion, finely chopped or grated
2 tsps. horseradish
¼ tsp. salt
¼ tsp. celery seed
½ cup pecans, chopped
3 T. parsley, snipped

☐ Drain and flake salmon, removing skin and bones. Combine salmon, cream cheese, lemon juice, onion, horseradish, salt, and celery seed. Mix thoroughly. Chill several hours. Combine pecans and parsley. Shape salmon mixture into ball; roll in nut mixture; chill well. Serve with assorted crackers.

PECAN STUFFING FOR TURKEY

Jeanne and Lou Rende

¼ cup margarine or butter
1–2 onions, finely chopped
1 cup celery, finely chopped
¼ cup parsley, minced
5 cups rice, cooked
½–¾ cup pecans, chopped
1 tsp. thyme
1 tsp. celery seed
1 tsp. salt
½ tsp. pepper
½ tsp. nutmeg
1 tsp. poultry seasoning
1 8-oz. can chicken broth

☐ Cook rice in chicken broth (adding small amount of water to adjust amount of liquid, if needed) according to directions on rice box. Sauté onion and celery in butter over low heat until onion is transparent. Remove from heat. Add rice, pecans, parsley, seasonings, and toss.

Yields stuffing for approximately 16-pound turkey. Also can be used to stuff Rock Cornish hens.

ITALIAN GREEN BEAN CASSEROLE

Jeanne and Lou Rende

2–3 T. parsley, minced
1 20-oz. bag frozen green beans, cut
½ tsp. salt
¼ tsp. garlic powder
½ tsp. oregano
¼ tsp. celery seed
¼ tsp. basil
¼ tsp. pepper
8–10 oz. Muenster cheese
2 tomatoes (or 3 small), cut into thin wedges
1 onion, sliced

☐ Cook beans 2–3 minutes less than according to package directions. Mix drained beans, parsley, and spices. Arrange half of the green beans in 2-quart casserole. Arrange tomato wedges on top of beans. Top with onion rings. Top with half of Muenster cheese. Layer remaining green beans. Dot with butter or margarine. Top with remaining cheese. Bake in 350° F. oven 25–30 minutes (cheese should be melted and very lightly browned). Serves 12.

This casserole can be made ahead of time and keeps nicely until time to bake it.

TEXAS ENCHILADAS

Patti and Bob Goodrich

Anyone who knows Monday Night Football's producer knows he is wild about Mexican food, and no one knows that better than Patti.

1 doz. corn tortillas
1 lb. ground beef
2 7½-oz. cans red enchilada sauce (hot or mild), to taste
taco seasoning packet or taco sauce in a can
1 lb. cheddar cheese, grated
1 lb. Monterey Jack cheese, grated
1 large onion, chopped
1 7½-oz. can black olives, chopped

☐ Sauté ground beef for a few minutes then add ½ onion, chopped and sauté until brown. Drain grease and add taco seasoning and ¾ cups water. Simmer 25–30 minutes.

In a skillet with 2 inches hot oil, dip each tortilla with tongs quickly on both sides. Then set aside on paper towels. Next, place each tortilla in a heated sauce and place in 9 x 11-in. baking pan. Fill tortilla with spoonful of meat mixture, cheeses, and a few olives. Roll tortilla and place side by side. Spoon sauce over to cover and add additional cheese, olives, and onions. Bake 350° F. for 20–25 minutes.

Mexican Version

Omit meat. Prepare tortillas in same manner but lay them out flat on baking sheet. Top tortilla with the two cheeses, then add another tortilla and cheese; then another tortilla and top with cheeses, onions and olives.

Top with sauce *after* baking. Bake 350° F. for 15 minutes. Serves 4–6.

QUICK HOT DIP

Patti and Bob Goodrich

2 7½-oz. cans Laredo brand chile (no beans)
1 lb. Jack cheese, grated
1 4-oz. can jalapeno green peppers, chopped

☐ Put chile in a pot and let it warm slowly. Add cheese and peppers, and stir constantly until cheese melts. Serve warm with tortilla chips.

Video operator Ken Amow was born in Hawaii. His wife Pat fixes Lau Lau to make him feel at home.

TACO SALAD

Patti and Bob Goodrich

1 head iceberg lettuce (or combination of romaine and other)
1 lb. ground beef
1 package taco seasoning
1 lb. cheddar cheese, grated
1 can pinto beans, drained
1 can black olives, chopped
1 large onion, chopped
2–3 large tomatoes, sliced
1–2 avocados (large pieces)
1 large bag corn or tortilla chips
1 8½-oz. bottle Caesar salad dressing

☐ Sauté ground meat until brown. Drain grease, add taco seasoning and ¾ cups water. Simmer 20 minutes. Let cool. Should not be runny.

Prepare lettuce for salad in very large bowl. Add first eight ingredients. Crush ½ bag of chips and toss in with salad. Top with ¾ bottle of dressing and toss. Top with another ¼ bag of crushed chips. Serve as soon as combining ingredients. Serves 4.

GAZPACHO LOS ANGELES

Patti and Bob Goodrich

2 16-oz. cans S&W tomatoes
1 48-oz. can V-8 juice
2 cloves garlic, minced
dash pepper
dash Tabasco
¼ cup olive oil
¼–½ cup red wine vinegar, to taste

Dice:
4 tomatoes
2 cucumbers, celery
3 green peppers
2 red peppers
2 zucchini
8 scallion

☐ Combine first seven ingredients in blender and blend. Add ½ cup of diced vegetables and blend until puréed. Cover mixture and refrigerate overnight.

Blend again for a minute when ready to serve and put in a large bowl with ladle.

Place remainder of diced vegetables in individual bowls for toppings for the gazpacho. Also may garnish with croutons and sour cream.

Serve in cups or small bowls. Serves 12–15.

LAU LAU

Pat and Ken Amow

Ken, a video operator, was born in Hawaii; Pat's specialty, Lau Lau, is a Hawaiian dish that makes him feel at home.

2 ti leaves (if not available, substitute grape leaf)
1 taro leaf (if not available, substitute fresh spinach leaf)
1 cube each beef and pork
1 piece fish filet

☐ Place beef, pork, and fish in taro and fold. Then place it in the ti leaves and fold, tying the ends of the leaves in a ball. Place in a steamer for about 90 minutes. Unwrap ti leaves and eat the contents. Serves 1.

SHRIMP CREOLE

Marge and Jack Hughes

Jack is an audio engineer, or "sound man." He's part of the crew that makes it possible to hear the announcers and the field action. What Jack likes to hear best, though, is Marge saying she's going to make Shrimp Creole.

5 lb. raw shrimp, cleaned
½ lb. bacon, diced
3 green peppers, finely chopped
4 onions, finely chopped
2 cloves garlic, finely chopped
4 cups celery, finely chopped
½ cup parsley, minced
3 1-lb. cans stewed tomatoes
½ tsp. black pepper
1 tsp. salt
1 tsp. curry powder
1 tsp. thyme
1 red pepper or ½ tsp. cayenne

☐ Sauté peppers, onions, garlic, celery, and parsley in bacon. Add tomatoes and seasonings and cook slowly 45 minutes. Add shrimp and cook 20 minutes longer.
Serve with rice. Serves 10.

ITALIAN SEED COOKIES

Marylyn and Jack Dorfman

Cameraman Jack says, "The best thing Marylyn makes is reservations," and after saying that he'll probably have to make these for himself next time. As Howard would attest, that's the price for "telling it like it is."

4 cups flour
1 Tbsp. plus 1 tsp. baking powder
½ teaspoon salt
1 cup butter or margarine, softened
1 teaspoon vanilla
1 cup sugar
3 eggs
milk
approximately 2 cups sesame seeds

☐ Stir together flour, baking powder and salt; set aside in large bowl or mixer. Cream butter. Beat in vanilla and sugar until fluffy. Add eggs one at a time, beating well after each. At low speed, gradually mix in flour mixture just until smooth. Chill dough in refrigerator about 20 minutes, turning occasionally. Have ready about 1" milk in small bowl and sesame in another bowl. On lightly floured surface, shape about ¼ cup dough in 10" rope, ½" in diameter. Cut rope in 2" pieces. Dip first in milk, then in sesame seeds. Bake in preheated oven (350° F.) for 20–22 minutes or until golden brown.

HAWAIIAN CHICKEN

Lois Filippi

Lois knows better than anyone that it's not easy being one of the few women on a mostly male crew. Traveling on the road and being "one of the guys" hasn't affected her ability to cook a great meal.

1 large can crushed pineapple in its own juice
⅓ cup orange juice
2 tsp. lemon juice
1 envelope onion or chicken bouillon
½ tsp. garlic, minced
½–1 tsp. chili powder
¼ tsp. ground ginger
1 bay leaf
1–2 tsp. shallots, chopped
1 tsp. Accent
1 chicken, cut into pieces, with skin removed
paprika
salt and pepper
fresh parsley, if desired

☐ Combine everything, except chicken, paprika, and parsley. Simmer ½ hour or so, to thicken. Put chicken in a pan with ½ cup water. Pour mixture on and let it stand ½ hour. Baste. Sprinkle paprika on chicken and bake for 1 hour in preheated 350° F oven. Baste pieces while cooking. And add more paprika. Can be served on rice. Garnish with parsley. Serves 2 to 4.

KIELBASI SKILLET DINNER

Olga and Stephen Nikifor

Steve, one of our cameramen, is a big man with a big appetite. Olga sends us this skillet dinner recipe she makes for him. Then she usually makes it again for the rest of the family! (Just kidding, Steve.)

1 27-oz. can sauerkraut
2 T. oil
2 large onions, sliced
4 cups fresh Mackintosh apples, peeled, cored, and sliced
½ cup white wine
½ tsp. paprika
1 Polish kielbasi ring (Boar's Head), pricked around

☐ Put sauerkraut in a large bowl; cover with cold water and soak about 15 minutes. Drain well. In a large skillet or Dutch oven, heat oil and sauté onions for 5 minutes or until lightly browned. Add remaining ingredients. Cover and simmer for 30 minutes, stirring occasionally. If there's excessive juice, remove lid 10 minutes before serving and turn heat high to concentrate juices. Serve hot, sprinkled with fresh parsley. Warm rye rolls or bread with cider make delicious accompaniments. Serves 4.

THE CREW

BOLICHI

Robyn and Drew DeRosa

Drew and Robyn love to eat. A visit to their house for dinner or for the day is always a guarantee of fine food and fun.

3–4 lb. eye of round roast
1 chorizo sausage (removed from casing), chopped
2 garlic cloves, minced
1 medium spanish onion, chopped
½ green pepper, chopped
salt and pepper, to taste
¼ cup olives, halved
1 tsp. Worcestershire sauce
1 small can tomato sauce
1 can consommé

☐ Cut pocket in eye of round. Mix all ingredients except consomméé. Stuff roast with mixture, forcing it to end. Flour stuffed roast and roast at 450° F. for 25 minutes. Pour consommé over roast in pan and roast at 325° F. for 2 hours. Baste throughout cooking time. Serves 4 to 6.

COFFEE CUP CAPUCCINO SOUFFLÉ

Robyn and Drew DeRosa

4½ Tbsp. butter
4½ Tbsp. flour
1½ cups boiling milk
6 egg yolks
3 heaping tsps. instant coffee or Sanka
½ tsp. cinnamon
⅓ cup sugar
⅓ cup coffee liqueur (Kahlua or 2 Weeks Viennese Coffee)
Confectioners' sugar and cinnamon for dusting

☐ Melt butter in sauce pan, and add flour to make a roux. Do not brown. Bring milk to a boil and add gradually; stir until thickened. Stir in sugar and instant coffee liqueur. Add egg yolks one at a time, whisking well after each addition. Pour into bowl, cover with wax paper and serve at room temperature. Can be held 2 or 3 hours. Beat egg whites until stiff and fold them into coffee yolk mixture. Pour into buttered and lightly sugared cups. Fill only ¾ full. Bake in pre-heated 400° oven for 15–16 minutes. Serve with sauce. Makes 6 cups.

Liqueur Sauce and Coffee
2 egg yolks
¼ cup sugar
2 tsps. instant coffee
1 cup milk
¼ cup coffee liqueur

☐ Whisk eggs until thick and lemon in color. Stir in sugar and coffee. Gradually add milk and cook over medium heat, stirring constantly until sauce coats a spoon. When cool, add liqueur. Serve warm.

COQUILLES ST. JACQUES

Robyn and Drew DeRosa

1 lb. scallops
1 cup white wine
3 Tbsp. butter
2 small onions (minced)
1 teaspoon salt
2 Tbsp. flour
⅛ teaspoon cayenne
⅛ teaspoon dry mustard
½ cup water
1 egg yolk
bread crumbs
grated cheese (optional)

☐ Wash and poach scallops in white wine for five minutes. Remove and cut into bite-size pieces; keep warm. Save liquor. Melt butter and sauté onions and mushrooms. When slightly browned, add spices and flour. Slowly add liquor and water, stirring until thickened. Add yolk and cook two minutes. Put scallops in shells or dish and pour on sauce. Sprinkle bread crumbs and cheese (optional). Broil until brown and bubbly. Serves 4.

DIJON CHICKEN

Tricia and Chet Forte

We figure cooking for our director, Chet, has got to be easier than working for him, but then there aren't 50 million people watching him eat! We have to give him a perfect show to make him happy! Tricia just has to serve him this.

1¼ cups chicken stock
5 lb. chicken (approximately), any pieces you prefer
salt and pepper
¼ cup butter
1 fresh clove garlic, grated
2–3 T. Dijon mustard
1 small onion, chopped
1½ T. flour
2 T. fresh parsley, finely chopped

☐ Choose a large skillet and melt butter. Prepare

136

chicken by sprinkling with salt and pepper. Then brown chicken slowly until evenly browned. On the side, mix remaining ingredients until well blended. (I save a little of the parsley as a garnish to sprinkle over completed dish.)

Pour mixture over the chicken. Cooking takes about 45 minutes on simmer. Turn the pieces regularly until tender. Place chicken on platter for serving. Take pan and stir all remaining drippings until slightly thickened. Spoon over chicken and sprinkle with remaining parsley. Serves 6.

RASPBERRY MERINGUE PIE

Tricia and Chet Forte

9-inch cheesecake pan (spring-loaded side or removable bottom)
2½ cup fresh raspberries (sugar to taste)
1 tsp. light corn syrup
⅓ cup water
1¼ cups sugar
4 egg whites
1 pt. whipping cream
1 package lady fingers, split
2 T. cherry brandy

☐ Place raspberries in electric blender and purée; then strain to remove the seeds. Add a little sugar if the berries aren't sweet. (You can use 2 packages of frozen berries instead, in which case don't sweeten because they are packed in syrup.) The purée should yield about 2 cups.

Combine in a small pan, water and corn syrup. Cook over a high heat until soft ball stage on a candy thermometer 240°.

Beat egg whites until soft peaks form and gradually add hot syrup mixture, for next 8–10 minutes beat mixture at high speed until the whole mixture cools. Add the purée of raspberries and the brandy.

Whip the cream until stiff and add to the other mixture.

Butter the sides of the pan and then line the sides with the lady fingers. If they don't stick to the sides, add a little more butter to the sides of the pan. Gently pour in the raspberry mixture, cover with a wax wrap and freeze.

Before serving remove sides of pan, garnish on top with extra raspberries and a dollop of cream. Even a mint leaf or two is nice. The pie looks nice and is light after a heavy meal.

"CRYSTAL PALACE" GLAZED HAM

Tim George and George Romansky

It takes three tractor trailers loaded with electronic equipment to produce and transmit the show every Monday night. Each series of production, tape, and maintenance trucks traveling together as a unit are called "Phases." Tim and George (the Doc), are the fix-it men for Phase Eight. From their maintenance area stocked with all sorts of tools, they are capable of fixing anything. They can also fix a cup of coffee, a hot Danish, or anything up to a glazed ham, due to the addition of a hot plate, a toaster oven, and a microwave oven. This may sound extravagant, but in remote locations, day or night, Anywhere USA, they have been lifesavers. Their area is a nice place to visit on a rainy day or for a five-minute break. It's been fondly dubbed "The Crystal Palace." Here, then, is "Crystal Palace" Glazed Ham.

3 lb. canned ham
1 8-oz. can pineapple rings
1 8-oz. can Maraschino cherries
½ cup brown sugar
½ cup molasses
½ cup honey
2 tsp. tarragon vinegar
1 tsp. prepared mustard
Ground and whole cloves
1-1080G Plumbicon camera tube (optional)
Allspice

☐ Mix juice from pineapple with brown sugar, molasses, honey, vinegar, and mustard. Heat over low flame until brown sugar dissolves. Season to taste with ground cloves and allspice.

Bake ham in oven at 350° F. for one hour. Remove, brush on glaze, and decorate with whole cloves, cherries, and pineapple. Return to 350° F. oven for 30 minutes. Brush on remaining glaze. Serves 4.

SOUPE À L'OIGNON GRATINÉE

Renée and Jesse Kohn

Originally natives of French-Canadian Montreal, Renée and Jesse taste a bit of home with "Soupe à l'Oignon Gratinée" (French onion soup).

4–5 large onions, sliced very thin
3–4 T. butter
¼ tsp. peppercorns, crushed
1 T. flour
3 10½-oz. cans condensed beef broth
3 cups water
(Or even better, 8 cups homemade broth, beef or beef and chicken combined)
8 slices French bread, toasted
½ cup Swiss or Gruyère cheese, freshly grated

☐ Heat butter in heavy-gauge saucepan. Add onions and crushed peppercorns and sauté until onions are light brown. Sprinkle onions with flour. Cook about 1 minute, stirring constantly, then add canned broth and water (or homemade broth).

Bring to boil, and then *simmer* on low heat about 45 minutes. Season to taste. Pour soup into ovenproof large tureen (or individual ovenproof bowls). Place toast slices on top and sprinkle with grated cheese. Place under broiler 'til cheese turns golden. Serves 8.

A guy like Howard Cosell, who takes great care with what comes out of his mouth, must also take great care with what goes in it.

Photo by ABC Sports

APPLESAUCE CAKE

Em and Howard Cosell

"The Coach" is always saying he had lunch with someone here or there and they told him this or that, so we asked him where his favorite places were across the country: San Francisco—*Ernie's;* Houston—*Warwick Club;* Cleveland—*The Theatrical;* Los Angeles—*Dominick's;* Pittsburgh—*La Mont;* Dallas—*The Mansion on Turtle Creek;* New York—*"21"* and *Quo Vadis.* Following are some recipes from Mrs. Cosell. She's found over the years that the best way to quiet

"The Mouth" is to put something delicious in it!

½ cup Crisco
1½ cups brown sugar
1 egg
1 tsp. baking soda
1¾ cup flour (approximately)
1 cup applesauce
1 cup raisins
1 tsp. cinnamon
1 tsp. powdered cloves

☐ Cream Crisco and sugar. Stir in beaten egg. Dissolve soda in applesauce. Add to mixture along with spices. Add flour slowly—enough to make a fairly thick batter. Bake in buttered loaf pan for 1 hour and 10 minutes at 350° F.

Keeps well for a week.

CREAM CHEESE–HORSERADISH DIP

Em and Howard Cosell

8 oz. cream cheese
4–6 T. sour cream
1 cup watercress, finely chopped
2 tsp. horseradish
dash of tarragon, mint, dill, and Tabasco

☐ Allow cheese to soften and then blend all ingredients.

Makes one jar.

SHRIMP ARNAUD

Em and Howard Cosell

1 T. tarragon or cider vinegar
⅓ cup olive oil
1 T. paprika
¼ cup strong prepared mustard
1 cup celery, finely chopped
½ cup scallions and their stems, finely chopped
¼ cup parsley, finely chopped

☐ This makes enough sauce for 1½ pounds cooked and cleaned shrimp. Marinate overnight.

CREAMED VEAL STEW

Ria and Zen Kocylowsky

The Kocylowskys sent us some of their old Ukranian favorites. The hardest part of this recipe is spelling Kocylowsky right.

2 lb. veal, in large cubes
1 tsp. butter
½ onion, chopped
salt
1 cup rice
1 T. butter
1 cup frozen peas and carrots
1 tsp. flour
2 T. sour cream
1 cup cold water

THE CREW

□ Brown the veal lightly in butter in a heavy pot. Pour in water almost to the top of the meat; add chopped onion, salt and cover. Simmer on low heat for 45 minutes. Separately boil rice in 1½ quarts of salted water. When almost done, drain water; rinse with cold water and drain. Place in a larger pot with a little water on the bottom; add 1 tablespoon butter on top; cover and heat in the oven 300° F. for about 30 minutes.

To the meat add peas and carrots and let it cook until tender. Stir flour into the sour cream; dilute with cold water and pour over meat. Serve rice in a deep bowl, garnished with the meat and gravy; serve a tossed salad or fresh cucumbers. Serves 3.

PYROHY

Ria and Zen Kocylowsky

4 cups all-purpose flour, sifted
1 tsp. salt
1 egg
1 cup lukewarm water
1 lb. potatoes
3 T. onions, chopped
4 T. butter, melted
½ lb. dry cottage cheese
3 T. butter, melted
1 cup sour cream

□ Sift flour with salt. Stir in egg and knead well by hand, adding water until dough is smooth, flexible and doesn't stick to the hand. Roll out dough to ⅛ inch thickness and cut out circles, using a 2-inch cookie cutter. To prepare filling, boil potatoes until done. Sauté onion in 4 tablespoons butter. Drain potatoes and mash with onion and cottage cheese. Place about 1 tablespoon of the potato filling on each round of dough and fold over in half circles. Seal edges. Drop into boiling water and cook just until water begins to boil again. Remove at once with slotted spoon. Place on serving platter and cover with the 3 tablespoons melted butter. Serve with sour cream. Serves 4.

UKRAINIAN POTATO PANCAKES

Ria and Zen Kocylowsky

8 large potatoes, grated
1 large onion, grated
1 egg
¾ cup flour
1 tsp. salt
¼ tsp. pepper
1 clove garlic, chopped very fine (or garlic salt sprinkled after pancakes are fried)

□ Combine potatoes and onion. Add egg, flour, salt and pepper; mix well. Add garlic, blend. Cook by dropping spoonfuls in hot oil in frying pan; fry until golden brown. Delicious spread with butter or served with sour cream. Serves 4.

Photo by ABC Sports

Jim Heneghan, pizza tester, is just as successful at developing his own recipes.

SHELLFISH STEW

Jan and Jim Heneghan

Jim, cameraman and food lover, sent a recipe for what he calls his "Lazy Man's Bouillabaisse." Jan likes it when Jim does the cooking.

In large kettle or stockpot add:
3 T. olive oil
2–3 cloves garlic, minced
½ cup each celery, green peppers, onions (green onions preferably)

Sauté until tender. Drain oil
Add the following:

2–3 #303 cans tomatoes, stewed, red, plum—any kind
1½ cups dry white wine
1 tsp. basil
1 tsp. oregano
¾ tsp. salt
½ tsp. pepper
pinch hot pepper or ¼ tsp. flakes
1 bay leaf

□ Cover and simmer 1 hour.
Add 1 lb. each, fresh or frozen, all washed and cleaned: Scallops (bay or sea scallops, cut in quarters); shrimp, small or medium; crab meat, fresh or canned. Simmer until done, 10–15 minutes. Serve with chilled white wine and crisp bread. Serves 8.

RESTAURANT ADDRESSES & PHONE NUMBERS

ATLANTA

Bugatti
Omni International Hotel
Marietta St. &
International Blvd.
(404) 659-0000

Dailey's
1700 International Blvd., N.E.
(404) 681-3303

Mary Mac's Tea Room
224 Ponce DeLeon Ave.
(404) 875-4337

The Peasant Uptown
Phipps Plaza
(404) 261-6341

The Pleasant Peasant
555 Peachtree, N.E.
(404) 874-3223

Sidney's Just South
4235 Roswell Road
(404) 256-2339

BALTIMORE

Captain Harvey's
11510 Reisterstown Road
Owings Mills, MD
(301) 346-7550

The Chesapeake Restaurant
1701 N. Charles St.
(301) 837-7711

Thompson's Seagirt House
5919 York Road
(301) 435-1800

BOSTON

Anthony's Pier 4
140 Northern Ave.
(613) 423-6363

Custi's
7769 Post Road, U.S.1
N. Kingston, RI
(401) 295-8732

Jimmy's Harbor Side
Northern Ave.
(613) 542-5600

Union Oyster House
41 Union Street
(613) 227-2750

BUFFALO

Alabama Hotel
Alabama, NY
(716) 948-9994

Frank and Theresa's Anchor Bar
1047 Main St.
(716) 886-8920

The Polish Villa
2954 Union St.
Cheektowaga, NY
(716) 683-9460

Salvatore's Italian Gardens
6461 Transit Road
(716) 683-7990

CHICAGO

Lawry's The Prime Rib
100 E. Ontario Street
(312) 266-7200

Nick's Fishmarket
1 First National Plaza
(312) 621-0200

The Parthenon
314 S. Halsted St.
(312) 726-2407

Pizzeria #Uno
29 E. Ohio & 619 Wabash Ave.
(312) 321-1000

Su Casa
49 E. Ontario St.
(312) 943-4041

CINCINNATI

La Maisonette
114 E. 6th St.
(513) 721-2260

La Normandie
118 E. 6th St.
(513) 721-2761

Rookwood Pottery
1077 Celestial Ave.
(513) 721-5456

R. Tapley's
124 E. 6th St.
(513) 621-7185

CLEVELAND

Captain Frank's
1000 E. 9th St. Pier
(216) 771-4900

John Q's Public Bar & Grille
Illum. Bldg., 55 Public Sq.
(216) 861-0900

The Pewter Mug
207 Frankfurt Ave.
(216) 621-3636

DALLAS

Bagelstein's
8104 Spring Valley Road
Northwood Hills
Shopping Center
(214) 234-3787

Blackeye Pea
5292 Belt Line Road
(214) 233-8227
and
4814 Greenville Ave.
(214) 361-5979

Casa Dominguez
2127 Cedar Springs
(214) 742-4945

Ianni's
2230 Greenville Road
(214) 826-6161

DENVER

Dudley's
1120 E. 6th St.
(303) 744-8364

The Eggshell
1520 Blake
(303) 623-7555

The L.A. (Last American) Diner
1955 28th St.
Boulder
(303) 447-1997

Park Lane Café
305 South Downing St.
(303) 777-7840

DETROIT

Brownie's on the Lake
24420 E. Jefferson
St. Clair Shores
(313) PR1-4455

Charley's Crab
5498 Crooks Road
Troy
(313) 879-2020

Fox & Hounds
1560 N. Woodward Ave.
Bloomfield Hills
(313) 644-4800

Joe Muer's
2000 Gratiot
(313) 567-1088

GREEN BAY AND MILWAUKEE, WISCONSIN

Del Mondo
1550 N. Farwell Ave.
Milwaukee
(414) 765-9330

John Ernst Café
600 E. Ogden Street
Milwaukee
(414) 273-5918

Hampton House
2750 Ramada Way
Milwaukee
(414) 499-0631

John Nero's
418 S. Military Ave.
Green Bay
(414) 494-2821

Mader's
1037 N. 3rd St.
Milwaukee
(414) 271-3377

HOUSTON

Captain Benny's Half Shell
7409 S. Main St.
(713) 795-9051
and
8018 Katy Pkwy.
(713) 683-1042

Casa Dominguez
3404 Kirch St.
(713) 529-5210

Nick's Fishmarket
1001 Fanmn St.
(713) 658-8020

KANSAS CITY

The Flamingo
801 N. 9th St.
Lawrence
(913) 843-9800

Jasper's
405 W. 75th St.
(816) EM 3-3003

Meierhoff's
3800 Broadway
(816) 931-0444

Remington
Sheraton Royal Hotel
9103 39th St.
(816) 737-0200

LOS ANGELES

Belisle's
12001 Harbor Drive
Garden Grove
(714) 750-6560

La Scala
9455 Little Santa Monica Blvd.
Beverly Hills
(213) 652-2827

Lawry's the Prime Rib
55 N. La Cienega Blvd.
Beverly Hills
(213) 652-2827

Man Fook Low
967 S. San Pedro
(213) 972-9467

The Wok
2808 W. Ball Road
(213) 826-3440

MIAMI

Centro Vasco
2235 S. W. 8th St.
(305) 643-9606

The Forge
432 41st Street
Miami Beach
(305) 538-8533

Marker 88
U. S. 1 Marker 88
Islamorada
(305) 852-9315

RESTAURANT ADDRESSES & PHONE NUMBERS

MINNEAPOLIS/ST. PAUL

Black Forest Inn
26th at Nicollit
Minneapolis
(612) 872-0812

Duff's
9th & Hennipen
Minneapolis
(612) 332-3554

Forepaugh's
276 S. Exchange St.
St. Paul
(612) 224-5606

La Tortue
100 N. 6th St.
Minneapolis
(612) 332-3195

Venetian Inn
2814 Rice St.
St. Paul
(612) 484-7215

Webster's
1501 E. 78th St.
Minneapolis
(612) 854-4056

NEW ORLEANS

Brennan's
417 Royal St.
(504) 525-9711

Broussard's
819 Conti St.
(504) 581-3866

Le Chateau Briand
Le Pavillion Hotel
833 Poydras
(504) 581-3811

Maylie's
1009 Poydras
(504) 525-9547

Moran's on the River
French Market Complex
(504) 529-1583

Tujagues
823 Decatur
(504) 523-9462

NEW YORK/NEW JERSEY

Archer's Ristorante
1310 Palisades
Fort Lee, NJ
(201) 244-5652

The Armenian and
Mediterranean Restaurant
210 Main Street
Fort Lee, NJ
(201) 461-5229

Chipp's
150 Columbus
NYC
(212) 874-8415

Dimitri's Restaurant
152 Columbus
NYC
(212) 787-7306

McGlade's
154 Columbus
NYC
(212) 595-9130

The Old Homestead
56 9th Ave.
NYC
(212) 242-9040

The Palm
837 2nd Ave.
NYC
(212) 687-2953

Tre Amici
1294 3rd Ave.
NYC
(212) 535-3416

Zabar's
2245 Broadway
NYC
(212) 787-2000

OAKLAND/SAN FRANCISCO

Boudin Bakery
156 Jefferson St.
San Francisco
(415) 928-1849

Ciao
230 Jackson St.
(415) 982-9500

Kans
708 Grant Ave.
(415) 982-2388

MacArthur Park
607 Front St.
San Francisco
(415) 398-5700

Scoma's
Pier 47, Fisherman's Wharf
San Francisco
(415) 771-4383

PHILADELPHIA

Bookbinder's
125 Walnut St.
(215) 925-7027

Ho Sai Gai
1000 Race St.
(215) 922-5883

La Famiglia
8 S. Front St.
(215) 922-2803

Marrakesh
517 S. Leithgow
(215) 925-5929

Ralph's
760 S. 9th St.
(215) 627-6011

PITTSBURGH

Al & Steve's 120 Bar
120 Federal Ave.
(412) 231-9029

Cornucopia
328 Atwood St.
(412) 682-7953

Grand Concourse
1 Station Square
(412) 261-1717

Le Mont
1114 Grandview
(412) 431-3100

ST. LOUIS

Belle Angeline
800 N. Wharf St.
(314) 231-4464

Catfish & Crystal
409 N. 11th St.
(314) 231-7903

Kemoll's
4201 N. Grand
(314) 534-2705

Stan Musial's & Biggie's
5130 Oakland Ave.
(314) 652-2626

Tony's
826 N. Broadway
(314) 231-7007

SAN DIEGO

Anthony's Fish Grotto
1360 N. Harbor Dr.
(714) 291-7254 or 232-5103

El Torito
445 Camino del Rio South
(714) 296-6154

Harbor House
831 W. Harbor Dr.
(714) 232-1141

Johnies Cheesecake, Inc.
(714) 263-2239 or 474-8424

SEATTLE

Canlis
2576 Aurora Ave.
(206) 283-3313

El Gaucho
624 Olive St.
(206) 682-3202

Elliot's Bay Fish & Oyster Co.
Pier 56, Alaska Hwy.
(206) 623-4340

Ivar's Acre of Clams
Pier 54
(206) 624-6852

Stuart's
6135 Seaview Ave., N.W.
(206) 784-7974

Tillicum Village Tours
Pier 56, Alaska Hwy.
(206) 329-5700

TAMPA

Bern's Steakhouse
1208 S. Howard
(813) 251-2421

Columbia
2117 E. 7th Ave.
(813) 248-4961

Fuji Steakhouse
6329 W. Columbus Drive
(813) 884-8120

The Kapok Tree Inn
923 McMullen Booth Road
Clearwater
(813) 726-4734

WASHINGTON, D.C.

C.K.'s
Baltimore-Washington
   International Airport
(202) 859-8350

El Tio Pepe
2809 M St., N.W.
(202) 337-0730

The Market Inn
200 E St., S.W.
(202) 554-2100

The Palm
1225 19th St., N.W.
(202) 293-9091

Rive Gauche
1312 Wisconsin Ave., N.W.
(202) 333-6440

HAWAII

Coconut Palace Dining Room
Coco Palms Resort
Kauii
(808) 822-4921

Island Holidays
2222 Kalakaua
Honolulu
(808) 922-6111

RECIPE INDEX

RECIPE INDEX

RECIPE INDEX